Happy Professor:
An Adjunct Instructor's Guide to Personal, Financial, and Student Success

By Erin Lovell Ebanks

Printed in the USA
Copyright © 2014 Erin Lovell Ebanks

ISBN: 978-1500505301

Table of Contents

Introduction: My Story

Typical Monday.

Wake up at 9:00 am, read a few surprisingly hilarious chapters from a travel book about Costa Rica while savoring my favorite morning ritual- an amazing cup of hot tea.

Jog over to the gym to take a cycling class with a girlfriend, hang out by the pool with her to chat for a while, shower, take a look at a TED video (TED.com) I heard about from a colleague (it's an awesome concept- I think we'll discuss that in class today to make the lecture more engaging), finally head off to work at 3:30 pm to teach my first of two classes today.

I'll have a smile on my face the entire 3 hours I'm at work, laugh with my students about every 15 minutes, be thanked by approximately 3 students, have my heart melted by at least 1 student who proudly shows new confidence and growth as a speaker, and be home to greet my husband when he gets home from work at 7:00 pm.

Does it sound like I have a cool part-time job? I do. I also make a decent salary that my husband and I can live on while doing something I would probably do for free, and most semesters I go in to work just 3 days a week.

———

Do you ever wake up in the morning, excited to start a new day and get to work? I would venture a guess that most people don't. I do.

I absolutely love my job and everything that comes with it. My friends and family would most likely describe me as one of the busiest, most content, and low maintenance (read 'cheap') people they know. I truly believe that my life as a part-time or 'adjunct' professor is largely responsible for that.

Yes, I have a great family who recently moved to my city, a supportive husband, and good friends, but I started teaching at a point in my life that my generation has deemed the 'quarter-life crisis,' and I have adjuncting to thank for getting me out of that rut during those post-college years.

I was in the middle of my master's program, I'd previously worked at a desk for 8 hours a day as a marketing assistant, I dabbled with the flexibility of being a blogger for a skin care company as well as for a tutoring center, and I worked as an intern writing photo captions for a city newspaper (the people I worked with were great, but the job just wasn't what I was looking for).

As different as each of these jobs may seem, despite the fact that they were all communication-based, given my college major, they all made me feel the exact same way.

Every day I waited impatiently as the minutes slowly passed, and like many people, I watched the clock until I knew it was time to call it a day. I didn't want to think about work when I got home, and I dreaded waking up in the morning to do it all over again.

Most importantly, I felt like something was missing.

Many of the people I've met have said they just don't feel fulfilled by their jobs, and I hope one day they find the type of job they wouldn't mind doing in their free time.

That's the type of job I have. I like to think that if I hadn't stumbled upon it as a teacher's assistant (TA) in graduate school, that I would have looked hard enough to find it later in life.

I believe that teaching college part-time has taught me the beauty of time management, it's taught me to keep an open mind, to never stop learning, to challenge yourself and others, and that the energy you bring to a group of tired students can change the classroom environment for the better. Not only that, but it's made me more appreciative of what I have and made me more satisfied with my day-to-day life.

Now before you start getting the wrong idea about me, I do know adjunct teaching isn't all sunshine and rainbows.

I've read the articles and blog posts written by frustrated instructors who call what we do 'abuse.' I understand that, for the most part, we're treated unfairly. However, I'm a silver linings kind of person, and I still get to do a job that I love.

Call me idealistic or naive, but I'd rather find ways to be happy about my job rather than constantly frustrated about it. This is one of those jobs you have ultimate control over; change your curriculum, change your perspective, and turn it into something you enjoy.

The 'angry adjunct' articles tend to leave me feeling defeated, so I choose not to dwell on those. I've looked for articles or books that show the positive side of adjuncting, and I haven't really found any that focus on the positive.

This is why I decided to put my own twist on things for those of you who want to wake up in the morning excited about teaching.

For those of you that feel the same way I do about teaching college part-time, or would like to, this is for you.

About the Book

Before we really get into things, let me tell you a little about myself.

My name is Erin Lovell Ebanks, and I'm an adjunct instructor at four local schools (it's quite a few, but definitely manageable).

I find my job challenging, exciting, and fulfilling every day. I've been doing this for five years now, and I've managed to make a career out of it and have some money left over to travel.

There are very few adjuncts I've talked with who have been able to turn part-time teaching into a somewhat profitable 'full-time' career, but I've lucked out and made some fortunate decisions at opportune moments that I think would be helpful to others in the adjuncting world.

There are a few people I have in mind while I write this book.

If you're fresh out of graduate school and aren't sure what to do now that you have a master's degree, whether you're 25 or 65, I suggest teaching a college class in your area of expertise one evening a week. It's a great thing to try for at least one semester, a great option to have if you ever need extra cash, and it's a potential makeshift full-time job if you can't help but fall in love with it.

(Call the community colleges in your area to find out when they hold adjunct interviews; the interviews are usually pretty laid back, with a convenient meeting place on campus for everyone who may be interested. The only requirement to teach is a master's degree- teaching experience preferred, but not required. Other times, searching for open adjunct positions on an employment website and submitting the required documents is enough to get you the job. I've been hired both ways.)

Mostly, I'd like to share what I've learned with anyone who's struggling as an adjunct professor, whether it be with overall life satisfaction, or how to manage students in the classroom.

I've shared my 'tricks' with other adjuncts, and even with friends who don't teach, but are surprised that I make a living exclusively from teaching- and are just generally interested in hearing how I manage it all.

I've been thinking about writing down my positive adjunct experiences as a blog and as an ebook for about two years now, since sharing some inspiring student stories and my positive outlook with family who urged me to share these experiences with others.

Spring just turned to summer, which means I've got a lot of free time on my hands, and it's time to put my thoughts on the web (you can check out my website at happyprofessor.com).

I hope after reading this short 'how to' guide for being happy as a part-time professor, you'll feel some relief about the long hours and little pay, and will be motivated to make a few changes that will result in this being that great job you always wanted.

Feel free to pass your copy of the book off to any colleagues you know who may need a boost.

Section 1
Getting Started as an Adjunct

Chapter 1
How to Develop Your Course
Effectively and Efficiently

Start Slow

If you're like many of the adjuncts I've met, you've received your master's degree and either couldn't find a job working in your field, or you already had the chance to work in your field and realized it wasn't as glamorous as it looked in the movies.

If that's you, and you didn't get to slowly familiarize yourself with the world of teaching through being a TA, I suggest finding a really nice colleague or two who will share their tips over a cup of coffee. I've done this more times than I can count, at various colleges, and it pays dividends.

I'd be happy to be that friendly face for you that can provide easy answers, and I'll be sharing as much general knowledge about managing the 'part-time instructor balancing act' as I can, but there are also course-specific, department-specific, and class-specific tips and regulations that you should be aware of.

You'll either need to learn about these regulations and course-wide requirements via the 'Faculty' section of your particular school's website (you can access it even if you're not employed there), making an adjunct friend, and/or attending any sort of faculty development classes offered at your institution.

I'll get into all this, and don't worry, you don't need to do all these things right away.

Lesson Planning and Collecting Course Material

When I started out as a TA in grad school, I taught three SPC 1608 Fundamentals of Public Speaking classes each semester in addition to taking classes, doing homework, and working on my master's thesis.

Luckily, I had the most unbelievable mentors.

I was taught how to manage a classroom by really kind women who had taught for years. They shared their online content, course materials, rubrics, handouts, lecture slides, and their experience. With weekly meetings to discuss how to manage a course, and also how to handle the unique student situations that inevitably come up, becoming a well-informed, well-equipped instructor came easily.

I was very fortunate.

One of my best grad school friends, who later became an adjunct after graduation, was not as fortunate. However, as you'll find many colleagues will do (if you've heard of 'C.A.S.E' in the faculty world- standing for 'copy and steal everything'- in the most legitimate ways of course), I basically handed over every piece of my course curriculum to her.

I've had enough experience teaching different courses in the past few years to know that if you ever need to borrow ideas and material from a friendly instructor, they're usually more than happy to help.

Develop a Course that Works for Various Schools and Teaching Modes

During my first 2 years as a TA, I taught 3 classes a semester and fully developed my course.

After graduation, I taught 4 classes at a local community college and tweaked the course to fit my needs and preferences since the department guidelines allowed for more freedom.

Feeling confident with my streamlined approach to teaching with a 'work smart not hard' attitude, I started working for additional schools each Fall and Spring semester.

I spent a few days each summer applying for open adjunct positions online and making needed changes to the course content that I'd been too busy to worry about during the school year. I finally felt I had built a solid course and was teaching a comfortable (yet fairly lucrative) number of classes.

So after year two of teaching post-graduation, I was working at a total of 4 schools (I think 3 is plenty for most people) and teaching 7 to 8 classes (any more, and you're asking for trouble) on average each semester, including summers.

At that point, I had very few changes to make to the course material each semester and easily converted most of it to online content, which made the transition to teaching at various schools as well as online classes fairly simple.

Take Necessary Shortcuts

You may be wondering how anyone can possibly manage to work their way up to teaching numerous classes with course content that you're satisfied with in such a short amount of time, <u>and</u> convert it all to work for one's online classes.

Here are some answers.

As you're developing your course, keep in mind what kind of streamlined approaches you can use to help you and your students most.

1. Visit the textbook publisher's website: The best way to create course content is by going to the textbook publisher's website. The website will have quizzes, lecture slides, and pretty much everything you might need. (You may need to contact the secretary of your department to get your instructor login and password to the site, but it's well worth it.)

2. Take advantage of SlideShare: You can also access lecture slides at SlideShare (slideshare.net). The other day I was searching Google for lecture slides about Hofstede's cultural dimensions for class, and most of the options that came up were from SlideShare. I had more than enough to choose from.

Whenever I'm asked to teach a new course at the last minute, the above-mentioned necessary shortcuts are my best friends until I can adjust the course and make it my own.

Provide Material to Students Effectively and Efficiently

The best way to organize course content for both face-to-face and online classes is by making it available to your students in different ways:

1. Email: Each semester I simply email my students what they'll need at the beginning of each unit. This includes reading material, directions for assignments, directions for speeches, grading rubrics, worksheets, sample assignments that show what I'm looking for, and my lecture slides.

2. Learning Management Systems (LMS): I provide the same electronic documents online through Blackboard, Canvas, Sakai, or whatever other LMS the school uses (that way students have no excuse for not accessing assignments and lecture materials).

It's also a time-saver to submit your students' grades here. I initially used Excel to record grades, but students want immediate access to their grades (and it took quite a bit of time keeping students individually updated) so I made the switch.

3. Paper copies: I make paper copies of all the electronic documents that I split up and staple together by course unit. I pass out these 'packets' for them to borrow during the class period while we discuss each unit, and they have electronic access to the same material when they go home; that way they have the option to print it themselves if they'd like to.

Many community colleges are trying to go 'paperless' these days, or at least they're trying to cut down on some of the printing teachers do, so relying on electronic access more than on paper copies for students helps me help them. I'm also able to save time by not making various trips to campus to print everything I need through the school.

4. Recorded lectures: I'm hearing more and more about the benefits of recording your in-class lectures. For online instructors, your students get the opportunity to watch and pause the recorded lecture as needed, which helps if they need to take notes or take a break.

I also like this idea for face-to-face classes.

I know you've all had this experience: a student walks in after the missing the class period where you gave a <u>really</u> important lecture, and asks, "Did I miss anything?"

Blank stare.

I know it's frustrating. Did you miss anything? Really? It's a tiny bit insulting, but it happens. Giving your students access to your lectures in video format would make them more accountable, and you wouldn't have to try to sum up your 20 minute lecture for late students in a single sentence.

Recording my lectures is one of my goals for the next school year.

From what I've heard from other instructors, the best ways to do this is to write a script for the lecture (this makes you sound your best in the video and is necessary for students with disabilities that may be in your class), use Camtasia (available at techsmith.com- you can use the 30 day free trial, or ask the secretary of your department if they have a similar program you can use, it's pretty pricey to buy yourself), and then load your lecture on YouTube.

I don't know about you, but I'm kind of excited to experiment with this.

5. Back up your material: Most importantly, I keep everything I need for my students on a personal flash drive/thumb drive (attach it to your keychain, otherwise I promise you will lose it), and I frequently back it up on a hard drive.

I reiterate: back it up on a personal hard drive. Not backing up all your long hours of work and those changes you <u>just</u> made to those lecture slides is a terrible mistake you only make once.

6. Learning Styles: Lastly, keep in mind that everyone learns differently. It saves me and my students some time and frustration if I incorporate activities and have them get involved with what we're learning (hands on/kinesthetic), incorporate lectures and video (auditory and visual), and use lecture slides and handouts that don't just include text, but sketches and pictures to help understand assignments (visual).

If I cover the basic learning styles, I know everyone's taken care of.

Teach the Same Course Each Semester

I highly recommend teaching the exact same course each semester for a few years, it's the best way to get a good handle on things starting out, and it makes the workload feel much lighter.

If you get bored one semester and the department you work for wouldn't mind you teaching a different course in your field, go for it if you feel you can handle it.

Mind you, it will feel like a lot of extra work in comparison to teaching the same class repeatedly (which may sound boring, but you can add some simple variety- like different videos and activities- so it's fun for each class).

Teach Content, Not Textbook Chapters

Fortunately, when I started teaching as a TA in college, the lectures I developed were content-based rather than chapter-based. For instance, I had a lecture to discuss 'Your First Speech,' 'Communication Theories,' 'Elaboration Likelihood Model,' 'Persuasive Speaking,' etc.

The various textbooks I'm required to use at each school always include these concepts; it's pretty standard for Public Speaking and Intro to Oral Communication classes. Each semester I make some minor changes (maybe incorporate some new movie clips or short instructional

videos on YouTube) and use the same basic
lectures.
Of course, sometimes I'll teach an interpersonal
communication course or something as specific
as Persuasion (this is where more seasoned
colleagues/friends have really helped out),
where I'll develop a few extra lectures, or I can
fortunately overlap and tweak some of my usual
course content.

Keep in mind, I don't jump at every opportunity
to teach a new class because it always takes
more time to develop than you anticipate.
However, when I'm itching to develop new
teaching material, learn a new subject, and I'm
up for the challenge, I look forward to
opportunities like these.

Chapter 2
Time Management and Organization

There are a few things that are important when it comes to time management, and there are things you're wasting your time with that you might not be aware of.

Procrastinate Wisely

Like most people, I have a tendency to procrastinate.

However, I've learned that putting things off and wasting time makes me feel much worse about the situation and can be extremely stressful.

As someone who teaches an average of 8 classes a semester, learning how to 'procrastinate wisely' was necessary for my survival. It seems like common sense, but I learned that it's okay to put off some of the 'to do' items I'm dreading as long as while I'm procrastinating, I complete an important task that I wasn't dreading quite as much.

How to 'procrastinate wisely' is something I figured out in college that greatly reduced my stress and guilt about being unproductive.

For example, just the other day I needed to watch 20 online speeches for one of my online classes. I really felt like I should, but deep down

I knew I was putting it off, so I looked at my 'to do' list (I'm a huge list maker, and I find it to be not only helpful but necessary) and attempted to work on some of the other things listed.

I tended to jump around and most of the items I attempted to complete didn't stick, but I was determined that I needed to do something on the list or I'd be disappointed in my unproductive day.

Then without even realizing it, I found myself in the middle of developing my Family and Communication course that would be starting shortly, and I had <u>really</u> dreaded getting started (but apparently not as much as watching those speeches- who knew?).

The task of developing an important foundation for that new class took me 6 hours, and I got everything done for that course that I possibly could. I even enjoyed it.

Sure, I didn't do the one task I felt I needed to that day, but who can feel bad about conquering the course material for a class they've never taught?

I was completely fine grading those online speeches another day.

Organization

You must be organized. This is not optional.

If you start out organized, teaching up to 8 classes will be relatively easy and fun (at least in my opinion).

I have colored manila folders for each class that I teach, with all the course information on the front (room number, meeting day and time, campus, title of the course). Believe it or not, when I'm juggling numerous classes, this gets me to the right place at the right time, and is needed almost every day.

Within the folders are papers I need to pass back, papers I need to grade, and a class roster stapled on the inside where I mark down attendance (I also have handy 'Graded- Pass These Back' and 'Need to be Graded' sticky notes inside my folder so I don't get papers mixed up).

One advantage of using flimsy little folders is that the displeasure of carrying around all those ungraded papers in something that wasn't necessarily meant to carry hundreds of papers, in turn, makes me grade and pass them back to my students quickly.

Your Location and Your Teaching Schedule

If you live more than 30 minutes from the various campuses you're working at, be sure to set up a schedule where your classes are all pretty much back-to-back so you're not wasting precious time and gas money traveling to and from said campus frequently.

If that's not possible, find productive things to do during the hour or two you may have between classes rather than leaving (you can use the 'But I need to grab lunch excuse'- which may take up those two hours- or you can bring lunch to save time and money).

Every college campus I've been to has an adjunct office that's rarely used (just ask, it does exist!), where you can get some extra work done during your spare time on campus.

Something else that will help you with time management is your permanent location. Think very carefully about where you choose to live.

The only reason I'm able to work at 4 different schools each semester (each with about 3 campuses around my area- and I do teach at all of them depending on the semester and where I'm needed) is because I live 30 minutes or less from each and every one of them.

Honestly, it was a complete accident that I chose to live where I did, but I would have moved long ago had it not suited my driving to each of these campuses.

Because of my location, I'm able to stop off at home to relax for a couple hours, have lunch, grade some papers, do housework, and even workout with a friend before I head off to the next campus.

Truly, the best thing I've done for myself in terms of time management and overall self-preservation is planted my home base smack dab in the middle of the route to each of the campuses I'm asked to work at.

The opportunity to go home between morning and evening classes most days makes a huge difference in one's day. It gives you a chance to truly unwind (and grab some lunch from your own fridge so you don't have to waste money eating out).

Get the School Email Sent to Your Smartphone

I used to spend at least an hour each morning checking email on my laptop, and it was a huge time drain.

I finally went online to find directions for having each school's email sent to my smartphone, which were actually outdated, so I called the Help Desk number on each school's website to accomplish this task.

Within a few minutes, I got email sent directly to my phone.

I now exclusively check emails when I'm at stoplights, waiting in line somewhere, or have a spare second. With the exception of sending emails that include an attachment, I haven't checked email on my computer in two years.

Have Standard Answers Prepared for Student Emails and Assignments

Make a Word document and/or a 'Notepad' page in your smartphone where you keep your common answers to commonly asked student questions. It saves a lot of time and frustration when you feel like you've answered the same type of email a dozen times that day.

If you teach online, keep a Word doc of common feedback you give to online students so you don't have to type out potentially long responses each time.

Look Into Online Teaching Opportunities at Local Colleges

One universal adjunct issue is that we are crazy busy during the fall and spring semesters, and left without work during the summer.

An extremely valuable thing you can do during those summer months is look into online teaching opportunities.

I had a colleague talk to me about how much she loved teaching online, so I searched the school website's 'Faculty' section, where she had directed me, and I found out I could take a summer class for 3 Fridays to certify me to teach online.

(I had no idea this was even an option, and I imagine other adjuncts are also left out of the loop. This is one reason to make friends at each school where you work. Unfortunately, many schools don't offer adjuncts the opportunity to teach online, but if you happen to work at one that does, I highly recommend looking into it.)

I was hesitant, but my colleague encouraged me to give it a shot.

With all the time I had to spare that summer, I not only took the class, but I also developed my online course and was teaching 2 online classes by the spring semester.

If that still doesn't sound worth it to you, consider a few things:

1. You will inevitably make valuable colleague connections while taking an online certification class.

2. You're guaranteed to save money, time, and energy by not having to drive to campus to teach (I usually teach about 4 online classes each semester, which requires approximately half the time and energy it takes me to teach 4 face-to-face classes).

3. You'll be offered additional classes because of the general lack of online instructors (initially, this was the main draw for me- tired of my classes being cut due to low student enrollment, I'm now asked to teach numerous classes each semester).

Like I said, I was hesitant to teach a fully online class at first, but the hardest part was creating the online modules.

I have no regrets. I'm more than happy to grade papers in my sweatpants.

Living in Your Car

As a part-time professor, you most likely work at various schools, which means you probably spend a decent amount of time in your car.

I've discovered things along the way to make frequent commutes more enjoyable and a better use of time.

I used to listen to the radio or talk to good friends on the phone while in the car, which was nice. However, I got sick of the same music being played on the radio and decided long talks with old friends maybe weren't the best idea while driving through my very congested city.

My best recent discovery: books on tape.

It's a great way (at least in my opinion) to calm your nerves and forget about your own stress-and you can borrow as many as you'd like for free at your local library.

Books on tape (aka audiobooks) may not be for everyone, but I find them relaxing, entertaining without being distracting, and a great way to sit in traffic without raising your blood pressure.

Of course, like any sane person, when I feel like listening to something I can sing along to, I break out an old favorite CD and bob my head while keeping rhythm on the steering wheel.

Making the Most of Your Time: My Experience

Warning: This section may not be suited for the faint-hearted.

I used to be a television junkie.

I was one of those children, then one of those teenagers, then one of those college kids who claimed I didn't have enough time to do this or that. Somehow I managed to be an excellent student, but I could have also had a much fuller life if I'd realized how many hours every day I was carelessly flushing down the toilet.

Like many TV addicts, I was in complete denial and chose to be unaware of the total amount of time I had dedicated to watching 'my shows' every day.

I was watching at least 4 hours of TV daily and spending an hour or so on any social media that had already come out (Facebook was pretty much all we had at the time, although watching numerous popular YouTube videos excessively and reciting them line-for-line to your friends was also in its heyday).

Then one day during grad school, a 'crunchy' guy I'd been seeing (he actually wore a hand woven man purse and introduced me to the wonder that was the public library- my long-term relationship with the library is one of the best things to come out of that short coupling) was eating dinner with me at my apartment and asked if I always had the TV on.

I was a little taken aback when he said it, but I'm forever grateful that he asked me that question.

Yes, yes it was. Always on.

I turned it off while we finished dinner, a little bit embarrassed about this bad habit I had never been aware of. For the first time in my apartment, there was no background noise of any sort, which felt uncomfortable starting out, but it was the beginning of a new me (I know that sounds kind of ridiculous and exaggerated, but it really was).

That day, almost exactly four years ago, is the last time I mindlessly watched TV.

I apologize for the long drawn out story, but I believe many people (although few will admit it) can relate. I like to believe I'm the type of person who's always lived their life with purpose. However, my TV addiction was something that somehow slipped through the cracks.

Now, if my friends or family want to watch a movie or television show these days, of course I will, but I wouldn't describe myself as a couch potato anymore.

I also don't aimlessly peruse social media. I understand that quite a few people in our generation use social media and blogging to make a living, but again, that has a distinct purpose.

It's important for people to keep blogs updated and check out other related social media and websites, but it's about practicing moderation. If I meet a new person who prefers social media communication versus texting, I'll use it to send a message to keep our lines of communication open, but that's the extent of it.

If I'm bored, I find something better to do.

Have you ever noticed that you really only feel like you've wasted your time as the end result

of mindlessly watching TV or sifting through
long lost friends' Facebook photos (trust me,
I've been there- how does that even happen?)?
I'm not a fan of feeling like I've wasted
precious time, so I stopped.

As a result, I'm able to teach more classes,
spend more time with friends and loved ones,
play my guitar, and read. I'm amazed at how
much free time I have now that I don't routinely
squander it away.

If you've ever wished there were more hours in
a day, eliminate the distractions. It's amazing
how quickly that wish can be granted.

Section 2
Your Success on the College Campus

Chapter 3
Networking and Faculty Development Opportunities

Befriend Your Colleagues

You know that professor that's just packing up to leave the classroom as you're walking in to set up? Potential friend. You know that new teacher that sat next to you at the last faculty meeting? Potential friend.

It doesn't hurt to say 'hi,' introduce yourself, and ask what they teach. Odds are, you'll see this person again and again. At the very least, it's a friendly face to greet when you walk down the halls, and at best, they may become your new confidant.

Attend Faculty Development Classes and Occasional Meetings

I didn't know the schools I taught at had faculty development courses for adjuncts until I'd been teaching for a year.

I also had no idea what they were or what to expect if I attended these courses, much less if I would enjoy them (the short answer, I've learned a lot and sincerely think they're valuable- a definite thumbs up).

Many schools offer these courses in face-to-face, online, and hybrid formats throughout the year. They're fairly short, condensed to be more efficient, and they set you on the right path for whatever it is you're interested in: Podcasting, Global Community College, Multimedia Tools, Classroom Management, Engaging Lectures, etc.

You name it, they've got it, and the classes are simple yet extremely beneficial.

At the particular school where I now take these courses every summer, you get a small pay increase and a more prestigious title: Associate Faculty member.

State schools and community colleges across the country have similar programs, just ask a colleague, the Dean of your department, or click into the 'Faculty' tab on your school's website and you'll be directed to a course catalog where you can choose to take the classes you think would be most interesting.

At some schools these faculty classes are few and far between, while at other schools it's like a huge club that you didn't know existed. Either way, it's absolutely worth your while to check it out and get involved.

The Benefits of Faculty Development: My Experience

To give you a taste of my own experience, the first time I heard about faculty development classes, I was fresh out of my master's program. I had a good grad school friend who was essentially my partner in crime during our first years transitioning into the adjunct world, and we shared every struggle and teaching opportunity with each other.

Our first summer as college professors, I got a faculty-wide email advertising a 5-week summer course for part-time and full-time faculty. It was an opportunity to make some extra cash that summer, which seemed amazing since she and I had little to no chance of being scheduled to teach a summer class this early on in our 'careers.'

Each of us applied to the program, which was really more of a formality, and we spent the next five Fridays visiting various campuses of this community college where we would also sit with our assigned groups to discuss ideas, theories, and the best methods of teaching.

It was eye-opening being introduced to different styles of teaching, different types of adjuncts and full-time faculty, what made them tick, what made them enjoy their profession, and what their opinions regarding the education system were. I met plenty of other faculty members who enjoyed teaching the way I did, and I was able to make valuable connections and exchange ideas with so many amazing people.

I can't pinpoint anything specific that I learned from these 4-hour a week sessions, but I know it was something I needed to be a part of, and I grew a lot as an instructor from attending these classes.

I loved the passion these people had for their fields, and it gave me a glimpse into my own future as a professor.

What kind of instructor did I want to be?

Based on my own observations, I was able to learn from these people what I was doing correctly in the classroom and what I needed to change.

Aside from learning how to be a better instructor, the most valuable thing I gained during this experience, and something I leave with each time I take a faculty development class, is at least one solid friendship.

I made a few acquaintances from this first faculty development experience, but the one good friend I made (who I still email and have lunch with on occasion) was a seasoned psychology professor.

She's free-spirited, happy, independent, and adventurous. In fact, she's given me lists of great places to camp and scenic areas to bike through. The stories and adventures she's shared about her husband and herself were what led me and my husband to go on similar adventures.

The topics she teaches in the classroom and the way she approaches teaching are progressive. Actually, she was one of the first people I knew who taught online mixed-mode classes, and she convinced me to take the plunge.

Being friends with her is so worthwhile, and I leave with a huge smile on my face after each of our lunch dates.

I've also had other valuable, memorable experiences that I attribute to being involved in faculty development. The following experiences were a result of taking courses last summer for my online instructor certification.

While getting certified, I reconnected with an accounting professor I had met during the previous summer (another connection that might be helpful if my husband ever joins the adjunct/full-time ranks teaching Business as he claims he will one day), and it was great to sit in the back of the room each Friday to quietly catch up and hear about his children's recent accomplishments.

I also met an adjunct in that class who was the same age as me, which is almost unheard of where I live. Like my young grad school friend before her, we traversed some new terrain as a team, this time creating our online courses together via helpful texts and meetups after finishing the faculty development course.

It's so much easier to take those scary steps when a helping hand is just a phone call away, and it's comforting to know other teachers are also trying to figure out the same things.

You can't get experiences like these from keeping your head down in the hallway, falling out of touch with people, or skipping every optional meeting.

Sometimes it's intimidating to get out of our comfort zone, be the new kid in class again and try to make new friends. I know it's not the best feeling walking in by yourself that first day, and I usually regret it during the walk from the car to the classroom door until I see other people flying solo waiting to make a new friend as well, or in the best of cases, until I see a familiar face I can catch up with.

The thing is, after it's all over and it's time for the fall semester to begin again, I'm so glad I took the time and took the chance to meet new people and learn new things.

Something I try to live by is saying 'Yes' to new experiences (as long as it's in everyone's best interest, of course) because that's the hardest part. I can't ever recall a time when I was happy I didn't try.

Finally, I know networking can sometimes sound too formal, and almost like a sort of manipulative friendship, but I like to practice networking at its best. By that I mean that I enjoy developing quality friendships with good people who I know I'll help out whenever given the chance, and hopefully would do the same for me.

As an important side-note, that grad school girlfriend of mine has since moved across the country, but we continue to trade teaching tips via text and we list each other as references at new schools.

So you see how these connections pay off and last for the long haul if you're willing to invest a little time.

I'm also glad I took the initiative to make friends with other instructors because there's a lot of turnover in the adjunct world, and it always helps to be able to chat locally with someone who understands your job, classroom struggles, and overall lifestyle.

Making and keeping connections with your colleagues, even from afar, makes the potentially lonely adjunct path a rather pleasant, social one.

Chapter 4
Adjuncting versus Full-Time Teaching

The Benefits of Adjuncting Rather than Teaching Full-Time

I know this is a stretch, and I realize many adjuncts are not too pleased with the lack of full-time job opportunities, but I'm going to share some of my 'glass half full' mentality with you and hope that some of it sticks:

1. You get to essentially be your own boss.

2. You can teach as many or as few classes each semester as you want.

3. Whoever hires you (quite often at the last minute- possibly to take over a class someone else was supposed to teach that semester) is usually pretty grateful. It feels nice to be the lifesaver.

4. You're not required to go to meetings.

5. You're not required to hold office hours.

6. You get to experience different types of students.

7. You're able to explore different methods of teaching. (Important note here, one of the schools I work at has decided against online speech classes, understandably. Another school

has completely embraced it and I teach fully online for them; it's fun and interesting being on the cutting edge of new education practices.)

Tips for Getting a Full-Time Teaching Job

For those of you who are hoping adjunct teaching will just be a quick stop on the way to full-time teaching, and it really is your ultimate goal, I understand.

I'm not full-time, although I've seen plenty of my friends accept full-time teaching jobs and I'll let you in on how they did it:

1. Be happy and appreciative being an adjunct for the time being. The Dean of your department and anyone who matters will notice that you're a hard worker, that you get your syllabus submitted earlier than anyone else each semester, have been evaluated positively by your students, and that you take those faculty development classes.

When a full-time spot opens up, you'll be at the forefront of their minds.

2. Work at a few schools, be reliable, and be well-liked. Full-time teaching jobs are increasingly harder to come by these days, but if you work at 2 or 3 different schools, you'll most likely hear of at least one full-time position in your field amongst those schools

approximately once a year, based on what I've seen in the past.
Apply for each of those positions, they tend to be filled internally.

3. It's who you know: Become friends with people who will pull for you. I know a woman in my department; she's sociable, smart, and incredibly kind. As the story goes, she became good friends with a fellow adult classmate while they were taking the same master's class one semester.

Little did this woman know, the other woman was the Dean of the department at the school she was, by chance, hoping to work at full-time. Less than a year later, she got the job (having qualified and interviewed for it) and they're still great friends.

I have another professor friend who also got a full-time job from a friend in authority, in a very similar situation.

Why haven't I followed my own advice?

It actually took me quite a few years to even consider full-time teaching opportunities. I was so relieved that I had managed to start my adult life on the right financial foot, while basically being my own boss, that I was afraid to let go of that.

It took me a long time to come to terms with 'settling down' career-wise, you might say. I've always liked the freedom of 'freelance' teaching (doesn't that sound nicer than 'adjuncting'?).

A very short time ago, after having a heart to heart with a fellow professor who I very much respect, I finally decided that if the right full-time teaching job came along, I wouldn't hesitate to take it.

However, I love where I'm at. I am absolutely, 100% committed to continuing my life as a 'full-time' adjunct, should that be the case.

Section 3
Classroom Success

Chapter 5
The Value of Knowing Your Students

Icebreakers

I know a few teachers who think it's a waste of time to spend the first class period doing what we call 'icebreakers' to get to know each other in the classroom, but I happen to think it's the most important thing one should do at the beginning of the semester.

This simple practice makes life easier and so much more fulfilling for you and your students. As much as I know students initially dread these first day getting-to-know-you activities, the result really does make everyone more comfortable, and a few laughs are inevitably shared.

A tip for teachers: Share some things about yourself with your students first- and don't be afraid to smile!- they'll still respect you, but they'll also see you as human, which is a bonus.

Here are 3 ideas to get you started:

1. The Toilet Paper Game: I play what I call 'the toilet paper game' on the first day of class each semester. I think it really helps the students get comfortable with each other, and it's fun, too.

What I do is bring two big rolls of toilet paper out of my bag and tell them, "I know this is weird, but I want you to pass around these rolls of toilet paper and just take as much as you think you'll need. When everyone's taken how much they want, you can pass them back up to the front."

Everyone looks at me like I'm a crazy person, but they instantly start laughing and talking to each other. They now have something in common: curiosity.

Surprisingly, most students have never heard of this icebreaker. There's usually one student in each class who has an idea of what they'll have to do with the toilet paper, but they don't normally tell anyone else, so I've been able to use it year after year.

I ask who thinks they took the most, who thinks they have the fewest squares, and I tell them that if they got more than 10 squares they can just pretend they got 10 (you'll see why).

Here are the simple rules:

For each square of toilet paper the student takes, they have to tell us something about themselves- a favorite color, sports team, best movie they saw recently, favorite food, what their pet's name is, etc.

We then go around the class one by one hearing fun facts about each student. It takes the whole class period, but I encourage them to ask each other questions as they do this, find things in common with each other, and by the end of the class period everyone's inevitably made a friend.

The goal is to get them comfortable and willing to share speeches with everyone for the remainder of the semester, so this first day activity helps tremendously.

2. The Name Game: I did this icebreaker in a few classes when I was a student, and I remember how comfortable it made everyone, so I tried it my first few semesters as a teacher along with the toilet paper game.

It's a great way to get the class to open up on day one, and it's always been one of my favorites.

The rules:

You give the students a minute or so to come up with an adjective that describes them and starts with the first letter of their first name, in order to come up with a fun nickname. As a student, I always chose Energetic Erin.

Then you have everyone go around the room and share, but as each new person shares, they also have to remember each person's 'adjective + name' who went before them.

By the time you get to the last student, this person has to repeat, in order, about 25 students' silly names (and of course, classmates bond over helping each other when they get stuck).

It's very time consuming, but it's a great way to get to know each other, and I highly recommend it for professors who have a hard time remembering names.

3. Pipe Cleaner Interview: I just heard of this one the other day and I really liked the sound of it (used by The Chatty Professor when she guest posted on the Speak Schmeak blog, if you're interested).

What this professor does is pass out pipe cleaners (remember those from elementary school?) to everyone in the class on the first day, and then pairs them up with a partner (you could also do this in groups if you needed to).

They are then asked to interview their partner by asking their name, major, hometown, and whatever else they'd like to ask.

Based on what they've learned about the person, they then get as creative as they can and bend the pipe cleaner they're given into something that represents the person they just interviewed.

After each partner has been interviewed, and the pipe cleaner has been fashioned into something (it might form a certain shape that represents them, or an object like a baseball bat, flower, music note, etc.), they stand up in front of the class, give a brief introduction of their partner, and show the class what they made with the pipe cleaner.

The pipe cleaner basically serves as something to play with, add some levity to the situation, and eliminate some of the speaker's tension. I plan on trying this one next semester.

Know Your Students By Name

I've gathered that knowing how to spell each of my 200 students' first and last names, how to pronounce them, and what their nickname is is a little odd. I promise, no one will expect this of you. I'm not sure why I have a knack for this, but I can see the advantages it's given me.

At the very least, know your students' first names and how to pronounce them, it makes them feel like they matter and that they're not just a face in your classroom. Most schools even have student ID photos available online with electronic student rosters that should be available to you; I've met teachers who study this the first week of classes to get names and faces down.

It seems like something that wouldn't matter that much, and I do know teachers who don't bother to learn everyone's names for one reason or another, but below are some huge advantages I've observed when students are aware that you know and use their name in the classroom:

1. They show up more often.

2. They approach you more often with any problems or trouble they're having in the class before they reach the point of no return (aka lose hope and/or fail).

3. They take more responsibility with the assignments because they realize you'll notice.

Advantages for you as the instructor:

1. You don't have to say 'Hey, you in the back' when calling on someone, which inevitably will make you feel more comfortable.

2. It's much faster and more efficient to record grades and keep track of excuse notes/emails.

3. You know who it is that's been emailing you.

4. It's a time-saver because you're not constantly trying to figure out who's who in general.

Create a Supportive Environment

I teach communication courses, so naturally there are one or two speeches that are required during the semester, and I realize that's scary for students, so I try to make the classroom a supportive one.

Regardless of what subject you're teaching, I believe the classroom should be a pleasant environment to walk into. It makes for a better learning environment.

Most students don't take the initiative to visit me during the required office hours that I hold at one of my schools, either out of fear or complacency (or a real understanding of course material). However, I've noticed that if I bring a few minutes of individual conversation and personalized feedback into the classroom, my students are more likely to contact me afterward if they need additional help or would like to discuss an idea.

As a result of figuring this out, I hold at least two 'workshop' class periods each semester where students bring in rough drafts of their speech ideas (it can be any assignment, really) and I help them develop a topic and some main points to focus on based on their own interests.

As an adjunct without an actual office (like most), I use this as individual time with the students to give personalized feedback, to help them realize that I notice the work they're doing (whether it's good or bad, it tends to make them a little more responsible in the classroom), and it gives them a chance to talk with others in the class as well as with me.

(You can also email the secretary of your department to reserve an empty classroom for you on occasions where you might want to hold a few actual office hours, or a particular student would like to meet.)

Remembering That I Want to Be Here: My Experience

I have to remind myself, every once in a while, that I need to make the effort to get to know my students, and that my attitude should reflect the fact that I want to be in the classroom. Even when I think I've got my positive approach in the classroom permanently under control, I occasionally have to take a step back and assume some responsibility if things aren't going the way I expect them to.

Here's what I'm getting at:

My attitude and energy as the facilitator in the classroom affects everyone else's attitude and experience.

You can make up all the excuses you want for why your students don't like you, don't care, or greet you with blank stares while you're lecturing at the front of the classroom, but you have the power to completely change this if you take an interest in your students.

I don't enjoy taking the blame when a classroom of students seems uninterested or unhappy in my class; it makes me feel like I'm slacking as an instructor, so I understand it's hard for anyone to admit you play a part here.

However, when I'm finally honest with myself, I know I have it in me to turn the situation around if I put in a little more effort.

About a year ago I started noticing that every other semester or so, my very first class of the day seemed to be the class that looked bored and watched the clock waiting to be dismissed. Not every semester, but the occasional semester.

I tried to blame it on the fact that it's the first class of the day, they're all tired and so am I. However, sometimes that first class of the day for me is at 2:30 pm. I couldn't very well excuse them or myself for being mentally checked out in the middle of the day.

I finally hit me: I'm the common thread.

I'm not typically in 'teacher mode' during my first class of the day, so I'm usually still concerned with other things and not all there, mentally, in the classroom.

Sometimes I teach up to 4 face-to-face classes in a single day, and classes 2 through 4 are good to go. I've got my engaged, ready-to-help-you-learn teaching 'hat' on at this point, and enjoying every minute of it. It's just unfortunate that the first class of the day doesn't get the best version of me.

Let me share a quick story, I went a few semesters not understanding why that first class of the day wasn't excited to learn, until I figured it out and took steps to correct it half-way through the semester.

I was giving a lecture when I was up in front of the class, trying to engage them in a fun and effective way when I realized no one was nodding in agreement, no one cracked a smile, and I actually didn't know much about these kids at all. I hadn't gotten to know these particular students the way I had gotten to know my other classes.

No wonder they didn't care to listen to me.

After that realization hit me, I felt a little guilty for not noticing this sooner. As far as I could tell, I had been the problem all along.

Now it was time to see if my assumption was correct, and if there was still something I could do to change it.

I started getting to that particular class 15 minutes early and being <u>engaged</u> with whoever was there 15 minutes early. During the first week of doing this there were only a handful of students who were in class early. I started making small talk with whoever would bite: Did anyone have plans for the weekend? Had anyone seen a good movie lately?

If was slow going at first, but after they realized I was actually willing to engage in casual conversation, those 15 minutes before class became very enjoyable for everyone.

I know as a teacher, we can get tired of talking with all of our students all day long (especially for all you adjuncts out there teaching numerous classes). We sometimes just want to get down to business and do the minimum that we're required to do.

I can't deny, however, that it was much more worth it to put in that extra 15 minutes of enthusiasm than to spend the minutes before class silently checking my email.

Improving the classroom environment was just more important.

The entire feeling in that classroom changed, people smiled more, students would stay after class and ask me for advice about grad school or share the books they were currently reading.

They, all of a sudden, just liked being there (or so I was told from the feedback I later received).

After a few short weeks, more students started showing up earlier to join in the conversation, and it became one of my best classes that term.

I can't believe it took me so long to realize (and I'm sure this won't be the last time I have to relearn the same lesson) that it was ultimately up to me what kind of class I wanted to teach: one where students practically stare daggers at me while I lecture, or one where everyone learns with a smile.

Chapter 6
How to Make Yourself and Your Students Happy in the Classroom

Give Constructive Criticism in a Way That's Easy for Students to Handle

I tend to give my students constructive comments sandwiched in between two pieces of positive feedback when I give them verbal feedback, and also when I write feedback on their graded papers.

Anyone who's taken a course in management has probably learned that this is an effective way to motivate employees while also correcting any problems. It wasn't too much of a jump to realize that this popular management technique could work just as well in the classroom.

When my students give presentations in front of the class, I use the same sandwich method afterward in front of the student's classmates.

I learned quickly that in a communication class where other students would benefit from hearing the feedback their classmates were getting, I would need to present the feedback in an accurate, yet sensitive way.

For example, "Wow, I can tell that you spent a great deal of time researching your topic, and that showed. That's excellent and adds to your credibility as a speaker. However, remember that your speech delivery is an equally important part of the presentation. Use more eye contact with the audience rather than reading from your slides, and use more dynamic, varied vocals in the future to keep your audience engaged. Overall, work more on the delivery, but your organization, details, and content were fantastic."

As a pleasant surprise, I've had numerous students note on their end of semester teacher evaluations that they liked the feedback I gave. They claimed it not only made them become more confident students and public speakers due to the verbal praise, but it also helped them see the areas they needed to work on without feeling that they had failed in any one way completely.

That was the hoped-for result, and I'm more than pleased that my overall goal was met.

Care

I know it sounds silly and kind of obvious, but you should care about your students.

If you don't, you probably won't enjoy teaching as much as the next person. If you care about students and show them that they matter, they'll usually care about your class more, which will make you happier to be there.

Listen to Student Feedback Throughout the Semester and Give Them Choices

In the faculty development classes I've taken, the facilitator usually emphasizes that we need to remember we're teaching college, and many of our students have lives, jobs, families, and are adults.

The key to helping adult learners is to make them part of the teaching process and give them options. Consequently, if a due date for a certain assignment can be made flexible, I'll ask students which of two class periods would work better for them, and we'll vote based on a raise of hands.

Giving them a choice doesn't negatively affect me or my students, so why wouldn't I let them have a say? In the end, it makes them feel more significant and a more important part of the classroom.

Overall, many of the changes I've made and kept over the years are changes my students asked for, and they've been more beneficial than I could have imagined.

Create Student Groups in the Classroom to Make Everyone's Life Easier

If you don't already have each of your classes split up into groups for the semester, I highly recommend you give it a try.

Early on, I had a hunch that splitting my 20 to 30 student classes into 5 groups would make my life easier and their lives easier.

That has turned out to be quite the understatement.

Before I go any further, let me explain how I do this. On the first day of class, after everyone's participated in an icebreaker, they've loosened up and had a few laughs, I look at my class roster and start drawing a line under each 5th person's name (the number of students in each group is never an even 5, and inevitably a few students drop the class, but having roughly 5 people in each group provides plenty of cushion for those cases).

I do this alphabetically as I go down the roster, it's the easiest way to split the class.
Normally I finish up with 5 groups of about 5 people. After I've split them up, and made sure they've looked around to see who their specific group members will be for the semester, I give them a designated spot in the room to meet together, exchange contact information, and get to know each other.

The benefit to students is noticeable from day one.

They seem relieved, less nervous, happier, and they have an automatic support system in the class. We're also able to effectively complete many in-class group activities throughout the semester because they're comfortable asking their group members for help if they're confused.

As I walk around the room during these activities to make sure everyone's on-task and doing things correctly, I have fewer questions to answer because between the five of them in this comfort zone they've created, they've got it all figured out.

Another benefit of groups for adult learners is that they're able to take turns leading the group, they have people to bounce ideas off of, and when it comes to group activities, they're able to be active during the class period. This helps break up the class time and keep them awake (most of these people are balancing more in their lives than you know, so it makes staying alert during the class period much easier).

The benefit to you is that when someone misses class or is confused about the content, they usually ask a group member for notes or clarification before they come to you, which in turn saves you time and frustration at having to repeat yourself.

I've also had students come to me at the beginning of the class period to tell me their group member texted them saying they wouldn't be able to make it to class, which keeps me from having to check up on them (they've already updated me). More often than not, that group member will even offer to fill their friend in on what's going on and what the homework will be.

When done right, delegation in the classroom can help you out immensely.

I've never had any real complaints from my students about being put in groups, but I've received a lot of positive feedback about it.

I started using groups in the classroom because I thought it would help me and my students in all the ways I've mentioned, and it turns out-based on conversations with students- that it did help in all the ways I was hoping, and more.

Give Students a Chance to Teach the Material

If you've decided you're going to try splitting your classes into groups for the semester, something else you might want to try is a group presentation.

What I mean by this is give your students a chance to teach the textbook material as a group in front of the class.

My graduate school professors had us do this all the time, and I can see how effective it was for both the instructor and the students.

Student advantage:

I've heard from students that it gets tiring listening to one person talk to you the entire class period nearly <u>every</u> class period of the semester. On the other hand, listening to your peers explain the content, in a way that they know will engage you and relate to you best, is sometimes more effective.

Instructor advantage:

Hearing your students talk about the course content gives you, as the teacher, a chance to observe what concepts they're struggling with, gives you a new perspective on how to approach the material, and as a result can keep your lectures from getting stale. In fact, many of the video clips and tutorials I now incorporate into my lectures were originally introduced to me as part of a group presentation covering the textbook content.

Like my grad school professors did, I'll fill in any blanks that were left out of the material when the students presented, which makes my lectures more concise and focused- and much easier for this generation's students to pay attention and learn what they need to .

Here's how to do group presentations:

1. Each group is assigned a few chapters: The group members are responsible for splitting up the textbook content amongst themselves and picking what material they want to cover. They are not responsible for covering all of it, they can pick and choose concepts that they like the most.

2. Visual aids:

a. Create PowerPoint slides (or Prezi, Google Slides, whatever works best for them) to present the majority of the information.

b. Incorporate some video clips and tutorials scattered throughout the presentation to show to the class, followed by a quick discussion and explanation of how the clip relates to the assigned textbook material.

c. Play a game (most groups choose Jeopardy) to quiz the class afterward on what they've learned. I bring candy to encourage students to participate, and for some reason giving someone a Jolly Rancher for a correctly answered question makes all the difference in the world.

3. Lecture portion: Each group member is required to prepare a few minutes of lecture material to present to the class (this is where the lecture slides come in), and group members must ask the class questions periodically, as well as reference page numbers where material can be found.

4. Delivery: They must be engaging, knowledgeable, well-connected to the class, and have a well-practiced delivery.

5. The presentation as a whole: In its entirety, the group presentation is 30 to 45 minutes long (students are timed and graded individually). While they present the textbook material, I jot down notes about content to explain further, or I'll make a note of concepts I'll need to correct any misconceptions about. I also write notes about the speaker's delivery. Afterward, I share everything with the class in a purposeful and respectful way.

So that's the basic way I've incorporated group presentations into the classroom, you may have to do a little trial and error to figure out what works best in your classroom.

I will admit, group presentations did <u>not</u> work well the first semester I tried them.

I had to figure out how to explain it better to the class, and how to get them to present the material in a way that would keep the class interested, but also teach them valuable information.

Telling them to 'get creative' in order to make the textbook content interesting did not work the way I wanted it to, probably because it was a little vague and wasn't actually part of the presentation requirement. I learned that I needed to <u>require</u> creativity on their grading forms (10 points for video discussions, 10 points for a game, and so on- that did the trick).

The required video clips, discussions, class-directed questions and very specific directions has turned these presentations into a chance for them to be the teacher, get some public speaking practice early on with the support of their group members up on 'stage' with them (I've been told this really helps reduce their nerves), and teach the material the way <u>they</u> would like it to be taught to them.

I do these presentations during the first few weeks of the semester, so it gives me some good insight into my students' personalities, learning styles, and needs.

Any professor of any class can use group presentations. I've found them to be beneficial in so many different ways.

Relate the Material to Their Lives

No matter what subject you teach, you can apply it to your students' lives in some way. Making the subject more relevant will, consequently, increase learning.

If you teach math, give a lesson about how to handle finances. If you teach English, have them submit a cover letter as an assignment for a job they're interested in applying for.

If you teach communication/speech courses, like I do, remind them that the skills they're learning will be needed in life whether they give a toast at a wedding, have to pitch an idea at work, ask for a promotion, or happen to be the PTA president when their kids are in school.

There Are No Stupid Questions

I've had students tell me they feel comfortable asking for help and asking questions in my classroom because I don't treat them like they're 'stupid.'

I don't know where they got the impression that I would ever do this.

I can't imagine any teacher would really discourage students from asking questions by making them feel that awful, but I do my best to make sure they understand that in my classroom, there are no stupid questions.

You see, I never raised my hand in high school because I didn't want the teacher to laugh at me or be frustrated if I had a wrong answer (so I guess I had the same fear as my students). My teachers weren't monsters, and I was a good student, but somehow I thought being laughed at was a pretty realistic outcome. As a result, I try my hardest to make sure I don't instill this fear in my own students.

I've had students ask me ridiculous questions, all teachers have had that experience, but I refuse to treat the question with disrespect. I just go with it. For all I know, a few other students had the same questions and were afraid to ask, or I may not have been clear, which caused them to ask the question.

I hope by answering the seemingly 'stupid' questions with patience that other students become more confident asking questions in my class and feel comfortable approaching me when they have a problem.

Basically, I don't want to be responsible for students feeling bad about themselves, discouraged, and confused.

As a result, I hope this will help them grow as confident, involved students, and hopefully promote more learning opportunities and a better learning environment. Isn't that the point anyway?

No One is an Outsider

You don't know what you're students are dealing with in their day-to-day lives.

Sometimes there are students that don't fit in or have a disability of some sort. Treat everyone like they matter. If you treat everyone in the classroom like they're just as good as the next person, you'll notice that troublemaker behaving a little better, that shy student becoming a little more outspoken, and you'll notice that lonely kid's group members take him under their wing.

Sometimes it just takes a few small, simple acts as the teacher to make the classroom a friendlier, more cohesive, and enjoyable environment for learning and growing.

Don't Judge a Book By Its Cover, Students Are Not Always What You Think: My Experience

On occasion, I've had experiences where I got a bad first impression from a certain student, causing my attitude to take a slight turn for the worst. In these cases, that negative energy can affect the entire classroom.

I've found that when you get to the root of those particular students' negative attitudes, or learn to ignore it (if you have no other choice), everyone else has a much better experience.

For instance, I had a student about a year ago who was openly unhappy to be in the classroom during activities and particularly when he got up to give his first two speeches.

After his second speech, I heard him mumble "I suck at this" under his breath while he walked back to his seat, so I pulled him aside after I dismissed the class for the day.

Beneath the frustration I could sense the despair, so I told him I would allow him to present his next speech one class period late, without a point penalty, if he agreed to come to my office hours after class for the next 3 class periods with certain speech preparation assignments I was going to give him. He didn't seem too responsive, so I wrote him a follow-up email as well.

I was shocked to see his response.

He basically told me about his worries and disappointments as of late. He had taken a few missteps in college- he didn't make the sports team that had initially been his reason for coming to this particular college, and this was affecting his entire academic performance as well as his self-esteem.

He was polite and sincere, and told me he would do what I was asking, although he didn't think he had anything significant to say, much less what it took to be a successful speaker.

After meeting during my office hours, practicing his speech for me, and getting his first good grade on a speech, he became sociable in the class and had a smile permanently plastered on his face for the rest of the semester- and during the remainder of his much-improved speech presentations.

He ended up doing very well in the class and he wrote a last email to me, after all was said and done, thanking me for making him believe in himself again.

Wow.

Students have told me I've helped them in the past, but it's still hard to believe that we, as college professors, can make that much of a difference. We really can.

As instructors, we have the power to build people up. Every instructor can do this, regardless of what subject you teach. People go to college to better their lives, and I think it's great when we can make them feel that they're doing that in the classroom.

I have at least one student with a similar story each semester, one who does a complete 180 in the course as far as attitude, motivation, confidence, and grades.

Sometimes those students who have a bad attitude or scowl in the back of the room are the ones who need someone to reach out to them the most.

A little encouragement can change their entire college experience.

Section 4
Personal Success

Tricks to Living Within Your Means and Being Fulfilled

These are some rules I personally go by to live simply, inexpensively, and make the most of my paycheck, but like everything else I've given you advice about, pick and choose what you like.

Chapter 7
Personal Satisfaction and Making Money - The Best Kept Adjunct Secrets

Teach Online

Teaching a few online classes will save you gas money, time, and energy, which in turn will give you more time to teach other classes.

The benefit here is that you'll get the same pay teaching online as you would face-to-face, and it's satisfying to learn new methods of teaching. Variety can be very fulfilling.

Depending on the school you work for, you'll communicate with your online classes using one of a variety of learning management systems (LMS). I've used Blackboard, Sakai, Canvas, and Moodle (I'm sure there are more, but those are the few I'm familiar with).

With the help of whichever LMS your particular college uses, your class becomes entirely paperless and your quizzes and exams are automatically graded and stored in the grade book.

It's just as efficient as it sounds.

Not only that, but you can borrow online lecture slides and quiz/exam questions directly from the textbook publisher's website to import into your course for student use.

I'm not as tech-savvy as I wish I was, but fortunately when I was certified to teach online, I was also directed to what I consider the 'faculty technology center' where the employees go above and beyond to help faculty members develop their online content for sometimes up to 2 hours, as often as you need.

The front-end work is by far the most time-consuming and difficult part, but after all is said and done, when you do the math, teaching online adds up to more free time and a bigger bank account.

Take Care of Your Health

Taking care of your health can improve your quality of life, and save you some money and frustration.

I used to get sick approximately twice a semester due to teaching so often and being generally exhausted. I usually just needed a few days to rest, but this also meant I needed to cancel class, which meant I didn't get paid.

In my personal opinion, you should do some research online or talk to someone who knows about natural medicine to figure out how to best take care of yourself. I've received excellent advice about staying healthy, and I haven't missed one day of class due to sickness in the past year because of some simple changes I've made.

If you're curious, various teas with health benefits, local honey, bee pollen, and 5-10 minutes of yoga are now part of my daily regimen.

Get a Fun Part-Time Job

I've met some instructors that have part-time jobs to fill the summer months or to earn more money in their free time during the school year.

I know a few adjuncts who teach 3 or 4 classes and also do communication consulting for businesses. One adjunct works at a classy retail store to get discounts on her wardrobe, and another gives tours of a local farm for kicks. Sometimes these part-time jobs even turn into successful business ventures, so it's the chance to do two things you love and make decent money.

Chapter 8
Know What You Want

If You Would Prefer a Regular 40-Hour Work Week, This Isn't For You

I know a few people who thought they could make a living as an adjunct professor, and absolutely grew to despise the profession as well as their students, before they made a happy home at a more traditional job.

I know people who made a comfortable living as an adjunct professor, took a job full-time with a school, then missed their adjunct days when they didn't have a traditional boss, had more flexibility in the classroom, and had a variety of students. I also know those who taught college, left for a desk job, and missed teaching like crazy.

Lastly, I've met the people who did the reverse: worked a usual day job and took a pay cut to teach, claiming to have made the best decision of their life.

Every person's story is different, and I can't tell you who you are or what exactly you want. Luckily, I'd experimented enough in other jobs to know that the one I have is exactly where I want to be.

The trick is for you to figure out what it is that
you truly want.

If You Want to Get Rich, This Isn't For You

Enough said.

I've embraced a slightly unconventional way of
living, adapting my interests and hobbies to
things that I can afford to buy and do for fun.

In my opinion, mountain biking, hanging out at
the beach, going on walks with my girlfriends,
and going to free movies in local parks is a
thousand times more fun than shopping, going
to concerts, and eating at expensive restaurants,
but that could very well just be me.

If You've Realized Teaching Does Not Make You Happy, This Isn't For You

Some people simply do not like managing a
classroom and can't tolerate students who
'don't care.' I understand that, and it's perfectly
fine to figure out what job you're passionate
about based on trial and error.

If You Need Absolute Stability and a Regular Paycheck, This Isn't For You

I will gladly take instability over the daily
grind.

I once read an article stating that many people today are opting to make a living from working at multiple part-time jobs that they enjoy (I believe one young woman was a dog-walker and freelance magazine writer), versus having one job due to having more control of the work and more overall happiness from these flexible jobs.

If that sounds like an awful situation and you can't understand why someone would choose that life, you may be happier at a different job with more stability.

If You're Frugal, Enjoy an Ever-Changing Schedule, and Dislike Sitting at a Desk- Good News!- This is the Job for You

The description above may sound like it would only suit a select handful of people, but I've found that most of the adjunct colleagues I meet up with have views that are similar to mine. They'd rather live inexpensively with an unpredictable schedule than be stuck in 'the grind.'

As always, I hope I haven't offended anyone with my opinions. Nearly all of my loved ones and dearest friends have more traditional jobs or own businesses, and I think that's wonderful and a very rich experience.

However, for those that dance to the beat of a completely different drum, let's continue.

Chapter 9
Experiment with Living Simply

Some of the following may sound like a stretch, but I absolutely eat up anything I hear about living simply, minimalism, and self-fulfillment, so I thought I'd share.

Minimalism

Minimalism is generally defined as living with only what you need, and it can be applied in whatever way works for you.

Whether you want to travel the world with only what you can carry on your back, live in a remote mountain cabin, or just live more simply, you can practice minimalism.

I've adopted some 'minimalist' tendencies by accident. You'll see what I mean.

A philosophy I've heard from some authors who embrace the concept of minimalism, and a philosophy I've adopted as one of my own, is that one shouldn't feel the need to have work 'over here' and then your actual life 'over there'.

As the old saying goes, "If you love what you do, you'll never work a day in your life."

Basically, your work and your life should be one in the same; your life shouldn't be something you try to enjoy after an awful day at the office. I know that's difficult for most people to actually do, but I think there's a lot that can be gained from striving for this in your life.

When I first read about this work-life 'harmony,' I knew I was on to something. Without question, I would teach college classes if I didn't get paid for it. It makes me incredibly happy, and it makes me feel great about my life and what I'm contributing (in some small part) to the world of academia.

For me it's about living a fulfilling life and helping people with the extra bonus of getting paid.

How great is that?

Mind you, I am by no means 'rolling in it ' (if that's what you're looking for as a teacher, I'm afraid you may be disappointed). However, it doesn't seem that my husband and I should be able to save as much as we do with him working part-time as an intern and my teaching 8 classes a semester for relatively low pay (by most people's standards).

The secret?

It's pretty straightforward, we only spend our money on the things we need and the things that truly enrich our lives. We don't buy anything to feel a temporary high.

It also helps that we live in a small one-bedroom apartment and buying anything else would kind of be excessive (the one bedroom plan is partially by design, it keeps our budget in check with low rent, a reasonable electric bill, and plenty of room for everything we need but none of the excess).

This isn't for everyone, and I'm under no impression that my current way of life and where I live is permanent. I'm human. I occasionally buy something I really don't need but can't bring myself to get rid of.

However, my state of mind will always remain the same: I'm okay without the excess.

Invest Your Time (Not Your Money) in Inexpensive Activities

My absolute favorite things to do are relatively cheap, or free.

At least twice a month my husband and I go see old movies at local parks, and we only have to pay for gas. We have movie nights with my sister and her boyfriend where we take turns making dinner and picking out a movie to watch from their DVD collection.

We ride bikes in local parks and on biking trails, read books in the park at dusk when the Florida heat is more tolerable, and we'll spend a full day at the beach playing in the surf, throwing the frisbee, and relaxing under our cabana. Now, if I can find a great deal online for dinner or kayaking, I'm not unreasonable, I'll spring for that.

The point is, be mindful of where your money goes and make it count.

As far as I'm concerned, I have everything I could possibly need. Regardless of how much money I might make, I wouldn't choose to go back to my days of living more extravagantly, I've just come to enjoy simple living too much.

Activities under $15 you might enjoy (I understand you may be unable to do some of these based on your geographic location, but if they're within your reach and you're looking for something simple and fun to do on the weekends, take your pick.):

Beach: Swim, build a sandcastle, read, surf, boogie board, paddle board, play volleyball, etc.

Lake: Grab a kayak (or borrow from someone, or share the cost of renting with friends), canoe, paddle board, or just relax in the water.

Park: The park is one of my favorite spots. You can workout, see a movie, jog, go on a leisurely bike ride, read, fish, inline skate, have a picnic, feed the squirrels, play a board game, etc. The possibilities are endless.

<u>Hike</u>: Get a good workout, immerse yourself in the outdoors, and reflect in nature.

<u>Snow Activities</u>: I've never lived in a climate that's cold enough to actually snow, so I'll base this on my yearly winter trips to North Carolina. You can build a snowman, get season tickets to the slopes to try your hand at skiing or snowboarding (just be sure to take advantage of it and go frequently), and ice skating is fun and relatively cheap.

<u>Movie and Pizza Night</u>: We have some of our friends over to watch a movie and order a pizza at least one Friday or Saturday each month (occasionally we'll throw a board game into the mix if we decide to get really crazy). It's a great way to unwind after a long week, spend relatively little money, and enjoy time with friends.

<u>Indoor Picnic</u>: I love these. I put our picnic blanket in the living room, make a couple sandwiches, light some fancy candles, and stream free Alfred Hitchcock movies available online. Perfect, cheap date night.

<u>Coffee, anyone?</u>: Meet up with friends at a local coffee shop. Instead of feeling the need to buy an overpriced lunch, opt for their best tea or

coffee, or order the huge cookie from the display case like I typically do.

Crafts: A few girlfriends of mine enjoy doing crafts, so we'll make flower vases out of jars, make picture collages on canvas, and my all time favorite is making Christmas ornaments (check out Pinterest.com- you'll never run out of ideas). If your crafts turn out really well (more 'hand-crafted at an art fair' and less 'Mommy, look what I made'), you can give them as small gifts which saves you some money.

The Farmer's Market: Okay, I'm cheating a little bit with this one, normally I spend around $25 dollars at the farmer's market, but it's a fun outing with a girlfriend plus grocery shopping, so it's kind of like you're not spending money at all (wink wink).

Read: Open up a book and enjoy. If you love travel like I do, but can't necessarily afford to do it often, read books and blogs by travelers. I swear you'll feel like you were there without being out a couple thousand bucks.

Learn to play an instrument: I can almost guarantee one of your friends or family members is looking for an excuse to get rid of some instrument they bought long ago thinking they would take lessons and really take it seriously. Borrow it, or adopt it if they're not interested in it anymore. I love playing my

guitar, singing, and writing music, but my
guitars were gifts or hand me downs, and I was
self-taught. All for free- at least on my end.

I'm sure you can think of more, just enjoy
yourself and be creative. You may be surprised
that how much fun you have doesn't necessarily
depend on the amount of money you spend.

Learn How to be Low Maintenance

You'll have more than enough money if you
can find more satisfaction in a low maintenance
lifestyle.

This means visit your local library, cancel that
gym membership (or really really take
advantage of it), and eliminate what you don't
need.

I have a reasonably priced membership at my
local gym, but I can come and go as it suits me
and I get two people in for free every time I go.

So guess what?

Two days a week I bring a friend and my sister
with me, one day of the week I meet my mother
there to catch up, and at least once a week my
husband and I go to the pool there in the
evening.

The benefit?

I release stress, stay healthy, and hang out with the people I care about without spending added money. Until I start neglecting it, I'll definitely keep the gym membership.

Now for the local public library, I can't believe more people don't take advantage of this awesome place.

I borrow DVDs and books from the library to mentally prepare for that day when my husband finally decides he doesn't need to watch and record his beloved basketball.

He needs cable. I don't.

Until then, it's nice to know we've got plenty of alternatives and could cut it out if we really needed to.

Fun (and Cheap) Travel: My Experience

I'm talking about what I call 'mini' vacations here.

I love traveling, and I spent thousands and thousands of dollars visiting different countries every year during college. I thought I had satisfied my travel bug during that time, but it came back a few years after grad school.

Don't get me wrong, I don't have a single regret and each of those experiences was worth the money and extremely valuable, but I'm (a little bit) older and wiser at this point. I feel as though I can find some cheaper alternatives and still feel satisfied.

I have a very hard time parting with money for travel, even when it seems worth it. However, I keep travel expenses in check with one simple rule:

My husband and I can spend the equivalent of one month's rent to go on an awesome trip, as long as the trip is jam-packed with activities and around a week or longer (you can see I'm somewhat strict with my 'one simple rule').

Last summer we went to Nashville and crammed everything you should possibly do in Nashville into our 7-day trip. As a musician myself, I needed to go to Nashville once in my life and do it my way. It was definitely worth the money.

This summer we went on a cruise to Cozumel. We live about an hour from two cruise ports, and we spent a little over half of our summer travel budget (includes your room, all meals, and entertainment- I'm sold). I think we'll be doing much more cruising in our future.

Camping. Ah camping.

This is one type of vacation I can really get on board with. As a kid, I was used to sticky, sweaty Florida camping during the summer. It was fine, but no way would I be okay with sleepless 90 degree nights as an adult.

Luckily, my husband is a skilled camper; he's very particular, and he knows how to do it right. He prepares awesome campfire food ahead of time, only goes in the best of weather conditions, and is very strict about not getting the inside of the tent dirty- three things you wouldn't think to care about, but it has completely changed camping for me.

We prefer it to be a little colder (for us Floridians) in the evenings, say 50 degrees, so that the nights are perfect and restful if you have quite a few blankets- and it gives you an excuse to make a fire which, let's face it, is pretty much the whole point of camping.

Let me emphasize this again, though:

The conditions have to be nearly perfect to have a good experience, and the weather can change immediately.

I recall one camping experience where it started downpouring out of nowhere and lasted for a good hour, which resulted in my reading a book in the car while my husband, thankfully, sat in the tent to keep it from blowing away.

He wasn't the happiest camper for the rest of that trip.

When you can do it right, you know how to
sleep comfortably (go all out here, we borrow
camping equipment from friends and family),
can get a toasty fire going, and enjoy the peace
and solitude, it really can't be beat.

I've had many a camping trip where I wake up
to a bird chirping right outside my tent, only to
realize I've been out for 10 hours and slept
better than any night in my own bed.
Nature can be a marvelous thing.

To keep things interesting (and not too hot),
we'll travel distances up to 5 or 6 hours north
on the Eastern coast to try out new camp spots.

I like to go to scenic places, with friendly locals
and plenty of places to ride bikes. Some of our
future plans include exploring the biking trails
in Hilton Head, South Carolina, camping at
Edisto Beach, South Carolina, and checking out
the sights in Savannah, Georgia.

Our camping trip two years ago to Jekyll Island,
Georgia completely won me over.

What an amazing place, and it was only three
hours from our home. We spent time on the
beach, roasted marshmallows, and brought our
bikes to traverse the many bike trails around
driftwood beaches.

A wonderful three-day, two-night experience for a combined total (includes campsite price, gas money, and food) of $250 for the two of us.

That's what I call a worthwhile 'mini' vacation.

Some people have no interest in camping, which I can understand. You can find other cheap trips if you look hard enough.

Go visit a friend or relative who lives far enough away to make it feel like a vacation. A year ago we drove just six hours to visit my aunt and uncle who have an amazing home, kayaks, and fishing boat in Key Largo.

I also have some great friends who live in cool places scattered across the U.S. I know that anytime I want a quick and relatively cheap getaway, I'll have a free place to stay for a week (of course, don't be weird and invite yourself, but take friends up on their invites when they ask sincerely- or make a trade and invite them to stay at your home sometime, too).

Travel and spending time with people that matter, now that's a beautiful thing.

It's the Little Things

Lastly, if you're still looking for something more after experimenting with reasonably priced activities and vacations, these two little things make a big difference in my day to day life:

1. Meet people who have a similar lifestyle

Making friends with people who enjoy reading the same books, would be happy to stay in and watch a movie, and have an untraditionally flexible schedule is a huge advantage when working as an adjunct, trying to live on a budget, and striving to make the most of your days.

One of my closest girlfriends is my neighbor who works as a wedding photographer on the occasional Saturday and has her days free. That means she's willing to make plans to go on a run or bake cookies while watching a chick flick between my morning and evening classes. It's a perfect set up.

Becoming friends with your colleagues is also a great way to meet people you'll be compatible with, and the best way to do this is by taking any faculty development classes available at your school. Not only will you learn how to become a more skilled adjunct teacher, but you'll leave with at least one new pal if you make an effort.

It's also okay if your dearest friends only have their evenings free, love going out to a nice dinner after work and taking extravagant vacations in their free time. I know some of mine fit that description and they're more than happy to meet me in the middle.

2. Plan something fun every day

Whether it's meeting for lunch with a friend, talking on the phone with a loved one during your commute, or having an indoor picnic with that special someone, try to do one 'fun' thing each day.

It may be something short and sweet, but I've noticed that having that one daily thing to look forward to- that's just for me- makes each day feel special.

Section 5
Inspirational Student Stories

We've talked about some tips for a happy,
efficient classroom and for personal success,
but in the end, it's the individuals in your
classroom and in your life that matter most.

One of the original reasons I wanted to write a
book was to show other professors how
amazing teaching can be regardless of your own
personal circumstances or misgivings.

I'm sure- even if you're at your wits end with
your students lately- that you can recall some
significant times when you know you made a
difference, and you took pride in a particular
student's achievements.

If you're drawing a blank, I completely
understand- we've all been there. Whenever
you get discouraged, you're more than welcome
to borrow some student stories from the
following section and adopt them as your own.

Hopefully, these will help you remember why
you started teaching in the first place.

Chapter 10
Unforgettable Students (Who I Sometimes Forget)

Each semester there are dozens (yes, dozens) of students who I get to know especially well, whose stories I want to etch in my memory forever.

Now, back in my first year of teaching, I was fairly certain I could easily do this.

I felt like I would always remember each student because every semester I really do get to know each of my students particularly well.

Little did I know, as the years would pass, and I'd continue to run into these familiar faces around campus and around town, that I'd start having trouble putting names to faces. I hate this. There were so many teachers throughout my college years that I considered friends and mentors, and I'd hate to think that they've forgotten me.

As a quick side note, I hoped maybe this was all in my head and other students would accept that us teachers might not always remember them- regardless of how awesome they were- but a young friend of mine confirmed that I was, indeed, very wrong.

One of my best friends graduated college last year, and during her last semester she raved about a young adjunct instructor of hers who she would chat with about course material and who she really felt was a friend and teacher who cared. She told me one short semester later, she tried to say 'hi' when she ran into him unexpectedly, and he looked at her like he'd never met her before.

This really bothered her because he wasn't just another teacher to her, he was someone who had made a difference in her college experience.

Ugh. Break my heart.

So my hoped for theory is incredibly wrong.

Here's the story that finally made me rack my brain (I've been wanting to do this for a while) to recall some of the most important student memories and write them down:

The other night I was at dinner for a family celebration and the young man who served us looked familiar.

I always think people look familiar, though, and most times it turns out I've never met the person. These days I think every person I run into used to be a former student, and I end up staring at them far longer than our society would deem acceptable (I would like to apologize to these poor, uncomfortable people).

Right around the time I was leaving the restaurant, some memories started coming back. I remembered the classroom in which he took the course, where he sat, the people he used to talk with, the conversations we had, his dedication as a student, and a really great speech he gave on Beagles (yes, the dog breed, but it was a fantastic speech).

I felt so bad that I had forgotten him.

This is where my story takes a turn for the better.

I couldn't let it go, especially after writing this book about how amazing I think my job and students are, so I ended up going through all my electronic rosters from each school I've worked with over the past years (I've never once used the old rosters, and even wondered why they remain available online for so many years, but it turns out they were a lifesaver).

Each name and semester brought back a flood of warm, significant memories.

I remembered some of the meaningful conversations I'd had with students who specifically stood out in my mind and on the list, and decided I would document them for myself and any other instructor who might need some encouragement- but I'll get into that in a minute.

I wrote the student I had just seen a brief email saying 'hey,' I did remember him, and that I hoped all was well.

The thing is. I teach speech, and it's a class that (hopefully) makes a person realize that their words can reach people. It's a powerful thing, at least it was when I was a student.

I remember all those life-changing moments when I was a student in speech class. Those moments that turned me into a more confident, capable adult. I've had students tell me they had the same experience in my classroom after facing their fears and excelling outside their comfort zone.

I'll never forget what my speech teachers did for me, and I doubt my students will ever forget their personal growth in speech class.

Whenever you start feeling overwhelmed by student emails, obligations, papers to be graded, and a hectic schedule, think about those students whose lives you may have played some small part in- it makes it all worth it.

Here's my list of inspirational student stories. They're short and sweet, but worth a mention:

(Names have been changed)

Dale:

This particular student needs a mention because he was in my class the first semester I taught after grad school. He asked me if I'd ever heard of TED talks and at the time, my answer was, "No I haven't, I'll look into those."

I can't believe there was a time when- as a speech instructor, mind you- I didn't know about TED.com.

Thank you past student for being the first to bring it to my attention! You changed my life.

Calvin:

Calvin was a determined, driven student. He'd struggled with a stutter his whole life, especially when he got nervous speaking in front of crowds. He and I would chat after class, and his peers thought he was great; they were always encouraging him.

Toward the end of the semester he told us all that through practicing his speaking in the class, he had the courage to interview for a job he'd been wanting, and he wanted to let us all know that he got the job.

Evan:

Here's another student who needed some work
on his speaking skills for a job interview. I
worked with him throughout the semester, and
the whole class gave him encouragement.
The last day of class when he turned in his final
to my desk, he told me he did really well in the
interview and he attributed his new confidence
to speech class.

Carla:

This student didn't need any help with her
speeches. She was dynamic, intelligent, and
always well-prepared.

However, I felt honored when she emailed me
recently to let me know she was graduating in
the summer and had been asked to give a
speech at graduation. She asked me for some
last pointers about anything specific she should
remember as far as delivery and content went.

The attached manuscript of her speech was
great, very few corrections needed to be made,
and I had no doubt her delivery would be
flawless. I was extremely proud.

Christa:

This dual enrolled student of mine gave perfect
speeches the entire semester. She was sociable

and friendly, but mostly focused on her schoolwork.

She emailed me a few weeks into summer some years back to let me know that she had graduated as valedictorian of her high school class, and speech class had helped her to feel confident and prepared while she was on stage.

Andrew:

I love it when great students ask me to write recommendation letters for them. It makes me feel like I have some control over getting them down the path they've set their sights on, toward a job or life experience that they absolutely deserve.

Andrew was my first student to ever ask for a recommendation letter, and it was for medical school. All the speeches he'd given were medically and psychologically-based, and they were fantastic. He deserved this letter of recommendation as much as anyone.

A few months later he asked me to write another letter for a different school because he hadn't heard back from the first. He was very gracious and apologetic, and of course I agreed.

Less than 24 hours later he emailed me back saying he didn't need the second letter after all, he'd just heard back from the first school and he'd been accepted.

Karen:

Just the other day I was on one of my schools'
websites and I saw Karen's story on the
homepage.

She had won a scholarship to study abroad in
Russia as a political science major. I had
worked on a letter of recommendation and some
other paperwork for her to get the scholarship. I
was not surprised when she emailed me to let
me know she got it.

When I saw her story on the homepage recently,
I emailed her once more to say
'congratulations,' and she promptly wrote back
thanking me for playing a part in her
accomplishment.

Michelle:

I remember Michelle as one of my summer
students a few years back, and I still say 'hi'
when I see her in the halls of one particularly
small campus where I work (I love running into
former students here where the community's so
tight-knit).

During the term she was in my class, she and I
talked frequently about her speeches, the two of
us worked to build up her confidence, and she
put in a lot of quality work. It was wonderful
watching her grow as a speaker.

A few semesters later, I was walking down the hallway when I saw a poster of her. It turns out she was running for a position in student government.

She got the position (which is probably why I see her on campus so frequently), and I can't take any credit for it, but I like to think speech class played a part.

Craig:

I was at my sister's MBA graduation when I noticed that the student giving a phenomenal speech on-stage looked familiar.

Luckily, I realized he was a former student of mine when he was just beginning his speech- this way I got to spend the last half of his speech with a proud, ridiculous smile on my face.

I was absolutely beaming, and I told the news to my family members seated around me.

He'd been an incredible, confident speaker the entire semester he'd been in my class, so it didn't surprise me that he had become SGA President of this particularly large university.

The cool part of this story happened a week later.

I was doing some grocery shopping when I ran into Craig. I saw a smile of recognition on his face as he remembered me as his speech teacher. We exchanged pleasantries, and he went on to say he'd given a speech at graduation the other day and, as his speech teacher, he had wished I could have been there to see him at the culmination of his public speaking experience.

Can you imagine how fun it was for me to tell him I had actually been there?

I told him I was proud, and that he did fantastic. He was happy, we parted ways, and I spent the rest of my day on a high.

Brad:

I like to tell my students that their speeches matter, and I really believe that.

These days I tell my students about some important life changes I've gradually made as a result of hearing them spread these important messages, particularly in their persuasive speeches.

As a result, I wear sunscreen every day, I'm an organ donor, I don't text and drive, I eat less fast food, I've given ebooks a shot and realized I really do read more as a result, and I also do yoga daily. My students' hard work and well-prepared messages helped make those changes happen.

Brad's surprising proclamation after one student's final speech had to make this speaker feel fantastic.

I normally have students give each speaker some verbal feedback after their speech, and Brad volunteered to share his two cents this time. He said that this particular speaker was very compelling; he always enjoyed his speeches, the quality of the content, research, and the way he connected with the audience.

He went on to say that he wasn't sure if anyone in the class had noticed, but he'd lost about 40 pounds over the course of the semester after making the decision to take better care of his health based on the speaker's presentation about eating healthy months earlier.

He said he'd like to thank him for possibly helping him live a longer life with fewer health problems.

The class was in complete shock. There's no way every single person in that room was not moved by this.

I share that story every semester now to remind my students what a difference one person's speech can make in someone's life.

Nancy:

Nancy's story is also memorable, although she didn't necessarily influence the class through her informative or persuasive speeches, but with her love of books.

It was our one-on-one conversations that really inspired me.

She was one of the few students I talked casually with in one particular class during a recent semester, and she and I talked about books. She recommended good authors, and I told her what books I'd become interested in.

One day she shared with us, during an impromptu speech, that she loved reading so much that when she went on trips she'd sacrifice luggage space- forget the spare set of clothes, extra pair of shoes, and added weight-she was taking at least 10 books with her.

Later on she told me and a few classmates that she'd already read all the books she was interested in at the public library, so she bought cheap books on Amazon now.

I know what you're thinking. She's really read every book in the public library that interested her?

This was a pretty bold claim, but I chose to believe her. As a result, I'm a much more avid reader these last few months than I've been in the past, and I don't see myself slowing down anytime soon.

Thanks, Nancy. You've intimidated and inspired me.

I'm on book 14 since meeting you 5 months ago (don't get too excited, some of them were 50 page ebooks).

Matt:

Similarly, it wasn't necessarily Matt's academic progress that had the biggest impact on the class, but his change in attitude.

During our icebreaker on the first day of class when students introduce themselves, I have some students who seem to share this information unwillingly and almost angrily (I blame it on nerves).

I just smile at them and play it off like it's no big deal. I've learned that if I give these particular students a week, they warm right up- and it was Matt that taught me this the first time around.

Matt was a student in class who, when sharing 3 pieces of information about himself, included one particularly endearing fact:
"I'm not a people person."

He did go on to expand a little bit, saying that he didn't want anyone to take it personally, but he wasn't 'big' on people, he was a scientist at heart, and he didn't enjoy socializing, much less speaking in public.

Well then.

It wasn't long after Matt was put in his assigned group for the semester that he became very cheery, saved seats for his new friends every class, and was more than willing to socialize. He even admitted to the class now and again how wrong his initial feelings about the class had been.

What I'll never forget is the day of the final.

While everyone was silently working on their final exam, Matt came up to the front of the room to turn in his finished exam.

He then proceeded to walk around the classroom shaking the students' hands who had become his friends (which was virtually everyone), telling them quietly how nice it was to have met them.

As he waved 'goodbye' when he got to the door, the students who were still seated and working waved back, and some even verbally said their goodbyes.
Matt is now a legend in my classroom.

I tell his story at the beginning of the semester when I inevitably have at least one student during the 'toilet paper game' claim that they're 'not a people person.' It's amazing to watch them change every single time.

Sarah:

Lastly, I'll share with you the common story of a student who was just plain scared. She was afraid she would never make it through the course because she claimed to go blank and forget what she wanted to say whenever she got in front of a crowd.

If you teach communication courses, this may sound familiar.

This is the story every speech teacher knows all too well, and in the best of circumstances, this student's struggles actually bring the whole classroom together in an effort to support and encourage him or her.

Sarah was a paralegal who was deathly afraid to speak in public.

She told me she sometimes cried when she had to get up in front of a crowd, and I had my fingers crossed that she would be able to get through the course.

I coached her prior to her first speech, sat in the back of the room ready to cheer her on with an encouraging smile, and I knew her group members were doing the same.

She had to stop and restart a few times, but we all encouraged her. Students offered supportive words like, "You're doing great, Sarah!" when she paused nervously during parts of her presentation.

About halfway through the speech, she found her stride and was good to go. No tears.

When she concluded her speech, the class burst into cheers and actually stood up to applaud her. I was deeply moved by their willingness to help another person find her confidence.

Sarah never doubted herself on speech days again.

Every student has a story.

I've had some incredibly bright, well-spoken students who told me they were so incredibly scared of public speaking that they were considering not graduating because they didn't want to take the required speech class.

I've had students that, for some reason, were incredibly self conscious as speakers, although they were fantastic in front of the classroom (this is when I make them record their next speech so they can be impressed with themselves).

These particular students just need someone to continually reinforce that they're good enough. In <u>any</u> classroom, students need this positive reinforcement to have the confidence to keep going.

I've had students completely make up content and definitions during their first speech (not a great first impression on the teacher), after which I talk to them privately and hear them quickly confess that they're clueless, scared, and would really appreciate some one-on-one help. This typically happens once a semester, the student does a little extra work with me to make sure they're planning and practicing their speech correctly, and they end up doing very well.

Sometimes a little extra help and attention is all they need to become a more responsible student.

I've received 'thank you's' at the bottom of final exam papers, and happy 'hellos' when former students see me around campus.

I can guarantee you not all students like me; you can't win everyone over and, of course, bad grades will inevitably happen in each class.

However, I'm trying my best to make a difference and to help those students who are

willing to meet me halfway, and I'm pretty sure
they're aware of my intentions.

Leaving on a Happy Note: Key Points to Remember

1. This isn't for everybody

My personal successes and experience are based on several factors and lifestyle decisions that have become easy for me to maintain. However, I've had to work at these things, they didn't come naturally. I had to invest the effort in finding my own personal success in a way that would make me happy.

It's your life, it's your time, and making an investment in yourself to find the success that you want will require effort. Everyone's journey is different.

2. You get out what you put in

Don't expect all your students to listen eagerly to your lectures and work cooperatively together the moment you set foot in the classroom. There's a lot of balance required between rules, respect, and kindness, and you'll have to figure out where certain lines need to be drawn. It took a lot of small, gradual adjustments for me to turn my classroom into the type of efficient and positive environment that it is today.

3. I've really just scratched the surface

By no means have I covered every way to achieve personal, financial, and student success as a part-time professor. These are just some ways I've found to personally achieve these goals in my life.

As I come up with more ideas to share, and more ideas that might work for you, I'll put them on my website at happyprofessor.com.

If you enjoyed the book and wouldn't mind writing an honest review on Amazon.com, I'd truly appreciate it.

If you have feedback about the book, teaching questions you would like answered, comments, or your own stories to share, you can contact me at erin@happyprofessor.com. I'd be more than happy to chat. See you there!

Happy teaching :)
Erin

Resources for Happiness and Success

This section includes a quick reminder about how to make the most of adjunct teaching, some resources for classroom and personal use, and lastly, some notes about how to use relevant video clips in the classroom (particularly for communication classes).

You can find some of the following tips and resources on my website at happyprofessor.com.

Enjoy!

In Case You Need a Little Reminder: Easy Steps to Being a Happy and Successful Professor

(Note: If some of this sounds familiar, the following section is made up of excerpts from earlier pages in the book. I thought it might be beneficial for you to have it in a nice, tidy list format.)

As an adjunct instructor with motivated students and a generally positive outlook on life, other professors (and people in general) tend to have one question in common for me:

How are you doing this successfully?

It's not always easy, but here are 10 tricks to being happier, and more successful, as a college adjunct professor.

1. Come into the classroom with a good attitude.

I have a long story I could share here, but I'll spare you. Basically, remember why you chose this profession in the first place. If you enter the classroom in a good mood (and stay in a good mood despite whatever else happens), I guarantee your students will be visibly happier, more motivated, and cooperative.

2. Be friendly and respectful of your students.

The more respect you give your students, the more respect you'll gain from them.

If you're approachable and friendly with your students, you'll most likely get more participation from them, more appreciation, and they'll be more likely to approach you with questions about course content.

The end result?

They'll be more successful as a learner, making you more successful as the instructor.

3. Delegate classroom responsibilities.

Not only does delegation make your classroom more efficient, and result in you having more time and less frustration on your hands, but it makes your students feel important and part of the learning process.

As a suggestion, set your students up in groups, and when the class has an activity, designate one person in each group to be the leader. If you have a small job you could give someone else during class time, make the opportunity available to your students.

Once the class gets used to this routine delegation, most students will be excited to participate.

4. Make lectures engaging.

Incorporate relevant personal stories, TED talks (check out TED.com), Khan Academy talks and interviews (Khanacademy.org), or movie clips as discussion points during lecture.

Just a quick break from some of the 'dryer' material can help keep your students engaged and happy.

5. Network with colleagues.

Making friends at your school will most likely make you more successful as a teacher because you'll be more socially satisfied, feel a sense of belonging at the college, you'll have someone to bounce ideas off of, and it'll make attending school meetings more pleasant.

6. Take faculty development courses.

Taking faculty development courses in the areas you're most interested in (ie. Global Community, Podcasting, Intro to Online Teaching, etc.) will teach you new skills, reinvigorate your drive as a teacher, and introduce you to new faculty members who are interested in the same areas.

7. Take care of yourself physically, mentally, and emotionally.

Do some sort of workout, meditation, or yoga at least twice a week to clear your head and boost your energy level. Also remember to maintain a balance in your life.

It's okay to work a lot (I know we all do), but be sure you're staying connected to good friends, family, and maintaining your health.

8. Learn how to live with less (this equals more money in your bank account).

It doesn't matter if you make 30k or 100k a year, I know people who make both amounts and complain equally that they need more money. It's not the money they're necessarily looking for, it's more satisfaction out of the simple things in life.

Trust me, it's a great feeling to see that bank account grow and not feel compelled to spend it all.

9. If you're bored with the content you're teaching, find a new angle. It's in your hands!

If you're tired of giving the same lectures, add a short video clip a few minutes in, and center a fun and relevant discussion around it.

You could also add a new lecture and eliminate an old one. You could even spend less time on some material you've focused on for the last couple of years and focus more on other content that's just as important but never seemed to fit in time-wise.

It's all you.

10. Take a break once in a while.

I know during semesters when I teach 8 or so classes, I'm not quite sure how I'm supposed to slow down when the summer finally comes. I've usually become so accustomed to being around students and working around the clock that I have a hard time putting on the brakes.

However, let yourself relax, and consider taking an actual vacation. You'll come back a more refreshed, better instructor.

Classroom (and Life) Resources for Professors

Community College Success by Isa Adney and communitycollegesuccess.com

Isa Adney has written a fantastic book called *Community College Success* (Amazon.com), and her website communitycollegesuccess.com is just as helpful for students.

When I go through phases where I start forgetting what it's like to be in my students' shoes, I pick up the book and read a few pages to remember what they're going through and what they might need.

I've told my students about the book and even played some of Isa's short 2-minute-long YouTube clips covering various helpful, relatable tips for succeeding in college-depending on what my students need at the moment.

Her motivational speeches at different colleges can be found on YouTube if you type in her name. I've had some students come up to me later in the semester to tell me how her speeches really spoke to them and encouraged them to succeed.

Ellenbremen.com ('The Chatty Professor')

This tenured-professor's website and blog is an excellent resource for you and your students.

She gives detailed tips on how students should successfully communicate with professors, and how professors can successfully answer tricky student questions.

It's been a very valuable resource for me, and would be particularly helpful for new professors.

Khan Academy (khanacademy.org)

I'm so jealous of math, business, science, arts and humanities, and computing professors.

The instructors of the above-mentioned classes are the ones who get to use this collection of amazing Khan Academy videos and interviews to help teach concepts in a fun, engaging way to their students.

Khan Academy is a pretty young organization, but they've become popular in colleges, and I believe they're really changing education for the better.

One video I feel any instructor, or person for that matter, can especially connect with is CEO of Burberry, Angela Ahrendts interview in the 'Entrepreneur' section of the website.

She talks about the importance of being passionate for the work that you do, and it's an overall inspiring conversation- plus, she gives a nice overview of what Khan Academy's all about while sitting with the founder, Sal Khan.

TED and TEDx

TED (Technology, Entertainment, and Design) is an absolute goldmine for all professors.

Not only are the talks perfect for public speaking classes, but the concepts talked about are so varied that any professor in any department can find numerous videos or clips to help punctuate long lectures during the semester.

I watch TED talks frequently in my spare time because I personally enjoy them. I consider them the lectures I missed out on in college because classes like that just didn't exist.

The talks challenge my own ideas, change my perspectives, and give me the opportunity to continue learning.

In my classes, I normally pause TED videos every few minutes to discuss the content with my students- I can actually see them painstakingly trying <u>not</u> to yell out their opinions while the video is playing, so the discussion is usually a very involved, quality one.

It's exactly what every teacher hopes for.

If you've ever looked for a way to get students involved, TED is the answer. Sometimes it's my best way to get the shy students talking.

You can find the talks on TED.com and they're also on YouTube.com.

<u>YouTube</u>

This well-known resource deserves some extra attention.

I use YouTube in the classroom to share relevant movie and TV show clips, great speeches from students at other schools, and there are also short educational videos to add to lectures.

Over the years I've stumbled across some great 'how to' videos for speeches, including some really concise and useful YouTube segments from speech coach Darren LaCroix.

If you type in some search words along the lines of what you're looking for (as an instructor in any field), you won't be at a loss for some excellent options.

The Great Debaters

The Great Debaters is a great resource when your students are getting into the unit on persuasive speaking, or if you just want students in any class to appreciate the privilege of getting an education. It works wonders in getting my students back on track when I feel they've been slacking.

Depending on how much time we have, or how much motivation my students need, I'll show parts of this movie toward the end of the semester or I'll show it in its entirety.

It makes my students excited to deliver debates and they actually take the required research more seriously.

I also have them write a paper after they watch significant scenes from the movie.

In case you're interested in trying this in your own classroom, here's the assignment:

I have my students write 3 pages answering 10 different questions about the ways they've identified with one specific character in the movie. They're also required to discuss how they'd like to develop the speaker qualities that particular 'debater' has, and how that character might want to develop one or two of the speaker qualities that the student has (to help boost that confidence of theirs).

I usually have a good handful of students in each class tell me the movie inspired them to be a better speaker, student, and person in general (and I can actually attest to the changes). At least one student each semester tells me they went out and bought the movie to keep them motivated while they finish getting their degree.

I initially felt guilty 'wasting' class time the first semester I showed the movie- in just one class as a sort of experiment for future semesters.

However, if there's one movie that'll get your students to change their perspective on school, hard work, and the privilege of being able to earn an education, it's *The Great Debaters*.

Books that Just Might Change Your Life

Below are a few books you might enjoy. They're not really for the classroom, but if you liked some of my ideas and my attitude toward life throughout the book, you'll like these:

Everything That Remains by Joshua Fields Millburn and Ryan Nicodemus (theminimalists.com)

If you liked my section on living simply, or 'minimalism,' you'll love this book. At the very least, it'll give you a new perspective on life.

The Minimalists published this memoir in December 2013 when they were changing their lives through the concept of minimalism. I enjoy reading nonfiction books and memoirs about other people's journeys and successes, so this book was right up my alley.

Everything That Remains is the perfect book to take some good life lessons from. I'll be the first person to tell you, however, that I take everything with a grain of salt- I'm a big believer in adopting new ideas from various people and resources.

I enjoy learning about a lot of different things from different types of people, and then taking away some good lessons that fit well in my life, or would improve my life.

When I tell people about my 'grain of salt'
approach, inevitably a well-known Ferris
Bueller quote pops into my head (although I've
never admitted that to anyone until now):

"-Ism's in my opinion are not good. A person
should not believe in an -ism, he should believe
in himself."

Basically, don't take my word for it that
simplicity and minimalism are the key to life,
and don't go get rid of everything in your house
after reading *Everything That Remains*.

Hopefully you'll finish it having learned some
good lessons.

The Happiness Advantage: The Seven Principles of Positive Psychology That Fuel Success and Performance at Work by Shawn Achor

The *Happiness Advantage* is a collection of
positive psychology research findings that
proves we can train our brains, at any age, to
see life from a happier perspective. By doing
this we'll be more successful at work and reap
incredible health benefits.

I discovered this book while I was editing my
own book, and I was so excited to see that I
wasn't the only one who believed that positivity
in the workplace (or classroom) can motivate

your employees (or students) and increase productivity.

If you think being positive is too hard, a waste of time, or just not possible for you, I encourage you to pick up this book.

How to Be Like Walt by Pat Williams

This book about Walt Disney's success is really something.

I debated over whether to get the ebook version or the print version, but I'd heard it recommended by so many people, that I figured it would be the type of book I'd like to pass along to someone else when I finished, so I ordered the paperback.

Great decision. I already have 2 people waiting to borrow it from me, and I would like to share it with my students, too.

It's a story about living your dreams, staying motivated, and the impact that one person can have on others. If that's not a great book for teachers to read, I don't know what is.

TED Talks for Professors

I've noticed that each time I meet up with colleagues to chat for a bit, we inevitably end up talking about which TED videos we use in the classroom and what concepts we use them for.

Occasionally it seems like us teachers have already somehow stumbled upon the same ones, but I've also been collecting helpful TED talks over the years from students. They're compiled as a list in my phone, so I thought I'd share it with you.

Below I'll include a brief description of how I use the talks in my classroom. After watching the talks yourself, I'm sure you'll see how they could be useful in your own classroom.

Talks to Increase Student Confidence

These are perfect when I feel my community college students need some inspiration and confidence to make it through the day, and definitely through the 4 years of school they may have ahead of them.

The following talks can work for any class, but they work especially well in college success courses, communication and speech courses:

Amy Cuddy: Your body language shapes who you are

The Skill of Self Confidence: Dr. Ivan Joseph at TEDxRyersonU *(found on YouTube, not on TED.com)*

Kelly McGonigal: How to make stress your friend

Sarah Lewis: Embrace the near win

Angela Lee Duckworth: The key to success? Grit

Julian Treasure: 5 ways to listen better

Best Talks for Communication and Speech Classes

I show the following talks when students have to give an introduction, demonstration, informative, persuasive speech, or do debates:

Mark Bezos: A life lesson from a volunteer firefighter *(introduction speech)*

Jack Silver: Hack a banana, make a keyboard! *(demonstration speech)*

Terry Moore: How to tie your shoes *(demonstration speech)*

Nancy Duarte: The secret structure of great talks *(good for any speech, particularly informative or persuasive)*

Joshua Klein: A thought experiment on the
intelligence of crows *(I show this to introduce
informative speeches, but it also has a
persuasive lean at the end.)*

Sherry Turkle: Connected, but alone? *(This talk
is great to show before persuasive speeches and
debates, and just works well in any
communication-related course. Before I play it,
I ask them: Is technology helping or hurting our
social skills? Is it connecting us or
disconnecting us from each other? I tell them
there's no right or wrong answer, and that
there's a lot of gray area with this particular
topic. I give them the option of covering this
topic in their persuasive speeches, and a few
students usually choose to do a debate on the
content.)*

John McWhorter: Txtng is killing language.
JK!!! *(Again, this talk is great to show before
persuasive speeches and debates, and just
works well in any communication-related
course. Before I play it, I ask them: Is
technology helping or hurting our writing
skills? Do you think texting is an evolution of
the English language? As I mentioned above,
these are just interesting ideas to discuss in a
communication class. I tell them there's no
right or wrong answer, and that there's a lot of
gray area with this particular topic. I give them
the option of covering this topic in their*

persuasive speeches, and a few students usually choose to do a debate on the content.)

Talks for the Soul

The following are great TED talks for anyone. They've really meant something to me, so I've shared them with friends:

Ron Gutman: The hidden power of smiling

Brene Brown: The power of vulnerability

Sarah Kay: If I should have a daughter…

A rich life with less stuff: The Minimalists at TEDxWhitefish *(found on YouTube, not on TED.com)*

Student Interviews:
What It's Like on the Other Side

I once heard a faculty development facilitator (he's an adjunct professor and long time high school teacher- now that's commitment) tell us that we often forget what it's like to be a student until we become students again in these faculty courses.

It's true.

He went on to remind us that sometimes we can get so used to our own policies and regulations that we forget about common decency. He shared some of his own stories about giving students the benefit of the doubt, and giving them the best chance possible to succeed in his course, even when it seemed circumstances were working against them.

This facilitator suggested we try out something he used in his college classroom: 'No Questions Asked' passes. Professors could pass them out to their exceptional (but also exceptionally busy) students. I then went home and, of course, made way too many in all neon colors.

His simple reminder to be human in the classroom was one I'll never forget (as you can see, it's been a running theme throughout the book), and I've since shared his stories with many other professors. (Mind you, I think most professors would agree that we truly have our students' best interests at heart, are fair in the classroom, and we all do the very best that we can to help them succeed.)

After that lesson, I added a new assignment to Module 1 of my online classes. I now have each student fill out a 'Personal Information Sheet' (asking why they're in school, what hurdles they've had to overcome, what they hope to gain, what their short and long-term life goals are, etc.) so I can get an idea of who they are as individuals.

Passing out a survey like this in face-to-face classes is a great idea, especially if you're not teaching a communication class where you can't help but learn about everybody.

It helps me, in particular, to feel a true connection with my online students. It's easy to forget there's a person behind the name on your computer screen, but reading each person's answers in this assignment helps remind me that these individuals are in college for a reason, and they have goals and dreams like anyone else.

In the following section, I'll include some insight about college life that a few of my former students were willing to share via email. You'll see that students really are aware and appreciative of the time and energy that we all put in.

(Names have been changed)

Jennifer

Year in school (if you've graduated, when was it):
Sophomore, getting my associate's in December 2014

What are your career plans?
Nurse Anesthetist

What is your major? Why did you pick this as your major?
Nursing. I need to go through nursing school and have the experience needed to be eligible for Anesthesia school.

Why did you decide to go (back) to college?
I needed to make something of myself and get an education for my career choice.

What are some of your short-term goals? What are some of your long-term goals?
Short term: To get my Associates degree and graduate with a 4.0 (so far so good).

What were the hardest challenges for you in going to college?
The commitment that I was putting in (5 classes at once). It was a lot to handle with a job as well.

Were there any obstacles holding you back? What were they?
Financial obstacles were a little tough to achieve, but I achieved a few scholarships to help pay for my education and I am working to pay for the rest.

What hurdles do you still have to face on a daily basis? How do you overcome those?
Daily life situations, getting to school and getting to work, having enough time for homework and having enough time for family as well.

How can your professors help make the transition back to 'student' a little smoother for other students like you?
Knowing that their class is not the only thing we have to worry about; we have so many other things to worry about in life, as well as other classes to study and do work for.

How have your professors motivated you (anything they said, how they treated you, encouraged the class as a whole, etc.)?
Some of my professors have tried very hard to care about their students and care if they pass or not. They stay after class to help you, or email you with answered questions right away. They have office hours to give you additional help if needed. They give you options on how they can help if you don't understand. They do not point it out that you do not know an answer or get upset if you do not know something.

How have your professors made a difference for you? Are there any ways they may have helped that they're not be aware of?
I had a math professor that was extremely helpful. I am not very good at math, and she went out of her way to make sure I understood how to do math problems with multiple math problems that she went over with me. She emailed me help when I needed it on homework, and really took her time if I did not know how to do a problem. She really cared if I passed her class, and she cared about my education.

What type of classroom environment and/or setup do you think makes learning most effective for you and other students (professor characteristics, method of lecturing, type of activities, types of exams, hands-on learning, any other methods of teaching and learning that you like in particular)?
I like different kinds of learning environments and methods because everyone learns a different way, and I think that a professor should know that. I think they should do all different methods of learning, like hands-on, visual with graphs and pictures, auditory (verbalizing the information), write it down, and ask the students separately how they would like to learn the information. In the end, the students are the ones that have to learn based on how the professor teaches.

What do you hope to get out of going (back) to college?
I hope to get a career that I love and the education needed to be the best in my field, and to have fun with my job. I want to like what I do and enjoy going to work everyday.

<u>Brittany</u>

Year in school (if you've graduated, when was it):
2nd year (graduating with my associate's next semester)

What are your career plans?
I have recently changed my path and am pursuing a future in teaching.

What is your major?
Sociology

Why did you pick this as your major?
People have always fascinated me and I have always been told I am easy to talk to. I originally wanted to get into Human Resources/Counseling.

Why did you decide to go (back) to college?
I decided to go back and finish because the retail management scene I had been in for several years was wearing on how I viewed people and the world in general.

What are some of your short-term goals?
My short-term goals are to graduate community college and pick an exact teaching path to pursue for the next 2 years during the rest of my undergraduate.

What are some of your long-term goals?
Become a teacher that is inspiring to my students. I want to be a teacher that students will remember for good reasons, and to be able to make a difference.

What were the hardest challenges for you in going to college?
More schooling! I hated school growing up, and years of more classes didn't peak my interest at all!

Were there any obstacles holding you back? What were they?
Yes. My job at the time didn't require a degree and the hours were so demanding that I couldn't take day or night classes. The hours of retail, and especially management, could range from 45-70 hours a week.

What hurdles do you still have to face on a daily basis?
Managing work, school, and family life.

How do you overcome those?
Time management is key. And having someone or a group of people there to support you and cheer you on is definitely needed! Especially on those terrible days when nothing seems to go right and you question if it's all worth it.

How can your professors help make the transition back to 'student' a little smoother for other students like you?
Most of my college professors have been great along the way. There have been a few that seem to be teaching for the wrong reasons or have a hard time relating to students, but most are great.

How have your professors motivated you (anything they said, how they treated you, encouraged the class as a whole, etc.)?
Teachers that remember what they had to juggle through college seem to be able to relate to students of any age. They also seem to be the ones that are willing to help and offer their assistance, however they can, for you. I appreciate a teacher who is able to adapt and relate to students, and offer positive reinforcements while also being able to give constructive feedback and not come across as rude or mean-spirited.

How have your professors made a difference for you? Are there any ways they may have helped that they're not be aware of?
Not too many have had a huge impact on me, but speech class was a positive experience. Even when the speeches were subpar, the instructor helped build confidence with everyone. Layering the constructive criticism and compliments were helpful to hear what we needed to work on as speakers.

What type of classroom environment and/or setup do you think makes learning most effective for you and other students (professor characteristics, method of lecturing, type of activities, types of exams, hands-on learning, any other methods of teaching and learning that you like in particular)?

Not having a professor stand behind a podium is a huge plus! Being made to feel like you're having a conversation with the professor and not just being lectured AT helps the messages sink in better and also keeps the class more engaged.

What do you hope to get out of going (back) to college?

Figure out and pursue what will allow me to help students at an impressionable age the most. Feel the accomplishment of finishing my degree!

Laura

Year in school (if you've graduated, when was it):
Graduated summer of 2014

Career plans:
When I receive my bachelor's degree, I am hoping more doors will open for me. I am current in Higher Education and would like a career change. I have always dreamed about going into fashion. The sky and beyond is the limit.

What is your major? Why did you pick this as your major?
Business Administration. I feel like with this degree it's not just geared to one area, it is broad and I can use it anywhere when it comes to a new career.

Why did you decide to go (back) to college?
I work in Higher Education and I counsel students on the importance of a degree. I was going through a rough time in my life and decided to take my own advice and go back to school. It's one of the best decisions I've ever made.

What are some of your short-term and long-term goals?
My short-term goals are to build an emergency fund, save for a vacation, and pay off my debt. My long-term goals are to graduate from

college, save for retirement, and have a meaningful career.

What were the hardest challenges for you in going to college?
The hardest challenge for me was finding and committing the time to go back to college, and my age was another challenge. I have learned you are never too old.

Were there any obstacles holding you back? What were they?
I wasn't sure I would have the social and family support I would need to stay motivated through school.

What hurdles do you still have to face on a daily basis? How do you overcome those?
In some classes, I wasn't sure if I'd be able to comprehend the subject, or if my mind would be capable, since I'm not as young as I used to be. It was challenging at first, but by developing good study habits, I was able to overcome some difficult classes.

How can your professors help make the transition back to 'student' a little smoother for other students like you?
Be patient, especially with older students. Coming back to school is very intimidating. It's a process, and we just get there a little slower.

How have your professors motivated you (anything they said, how they treated you, encouraged the class as a whole, etc.)? I had some great professor that kept me as well as the class encourage and motivated.
With most of my professors, they've treated us with respect as adults. The communication was always open, and they were there to help us in any way.

How have your professors made a difference for you? Are there any ways they may have helped that they're not be aware of?
Professors have a lot of experience in the field you may be interested in. I have taken a few of my professors' business cards, and that's a great resource for networking. Whether he or she knows someone who can help you acquire your dream job, or someone who works at your favorite company, asking your professor to put you in contact with someone they know can be helpful in your career.

What type of classroom environment and/or setup do you think made learning most effective for you and other students (professor attributes, lectures, activities, exams, hands-on learning, any other methods of teaching and learning that you like in particular)?
I enjoy a classroom with a sense of excitement or discovery, and the chance to make mistakes and learn from them.

What do you hope to get out of going back to college?
A career that I love and a sense of accomplishment.

<u>Warren</u>

Year in school (if you've graduated, when was it):
Sophomore

What is your major? Why did you pick this as your major?
Public Relations/Advertising. Public Relations has always been interesting to me. I am deeply intrigued by how one promotes a public image, message or even a product, possibly working with a government agency or even a celebrity.

Why did you decide to go (back) to college?
At 31 years old, I honestly went back to school because I knew how important it was to set an example for my children. Also, my kids' homework was getting harder and harder, so I didn't really have a choice.

What are some of your short-term and long-term goals?
My short-term goals are to start my bachelor's degree, and long-term I plan to find a great job with a company I can retire with, and that pays well. I want to be able to provide my family with what they need.

What were the hardest challenges for you in going to college?
Working around everyone's schedules is not easy with kids. Also, trying to remember

everything I learned in high school was a bit of a challenge.

Were there any obstacles holding you back? What were they?
Not really, I figured out how to make it all happen once I made my mind up. It helps that there are many classes and times to choose from, especially when first starting your degree.

What hurdles do you still have to face on a daily basis? How do you overcome those?
Time management is my biggest hurdle. I manage to make it all work with a giant calendar on my wall. It also helps to have my oldest watch over my youngest when I need to study.

How can your professors help make the transition back to 'student' a little smoother for other students like you?
I like when a professor has everyone chat, learn each others' names, likes, and ages. You find you're never the oldest in the class, and everyone has their own obstacles to face.

How have your professors motivated you (anything they said, how they treated you, encouraged the class as a whole, etc.)?
I have had professors that did not say much to anyone. And I have had professors that you would swear were family. Telling a student, "I know you'll do great," when you can tell it's sincere really makes a huge impact.

How have your professors made a difference for you? Are there any ways they may have helped that they're not be aware of?
Luckily, I've had many great professors, and I'm thankful for that. They've made a difference for me by establishing a good learning foundation, so that my next classes are so much easier. It's important to me because, for instance, if I hadn't had a fantastic math teacher, physics would have been a harder class because of it.

What type of classroom environment and/or setup do you think made learning most effective for you and other students (professor attributes, lectures, activities, exams, hands-on learning, any other methods of teaching and learning that you like in particular)?
I've always thought hands-on learning was good for everyone; it's definitely best for me.

What do you hope to get out of going back to college?
I am hoping to gain valuable skills that I can apply to my life now and in the future, as well as a sense of confidence knowing that I went back to school and did the best that I could do.

Amy

Year in school (if you've graduated, when was it):
Graduated summer 2014

Career plans:
R.N. (Registered Nurse)

What is your major? Why did you pick this as your major?
A.S. Nursing. I picked this major because I enjoy taking care of people and making a difference in people's lives.

Why did you decide to go (back) to college?
After taking two years off from college, I realized I didn't want to get stuck serving tables all of my life, so I built up the courage and determination to go back to school. I'm more focused than ever now. Taking time off is not always a bad thing; it can provide you with a clear perspective on life.

What are some of your short-term and long-term goals?
My short-term goals are to pass my Nursing pre-reqs with A's and B's by Summer of next year, form a habit of working out regularly and eating healthy, as well as make more time for myself.

What were the hardest challenges for you in going to college?
The hardest challenges a few years ago, fresh out of high school, were finding motivation and a clear career path that I wanted to follow. Now, my challenge is to not be afraid of my potential. I realize, now, that I have endless amounts of potential, as we all do!

Were there any obstacles holding you back? What were they?
Yes, there was a death in my family, which made it hard for me to concentrate on school and other aspects of my life; that was the reason I took time off from school. However, I was able to get over that hurdle enough to focus on school again.

What hurdles do you still have to face on a daily basis? How do you overcome those?
As every human experiences, I come across lack of motivation and lack of confidence within myself. I sometimes think, "Oh, what am I thinking? I can't do it, that goal is out of my reach." Yet, I have to remind myself that it's just my brain playing tricks on me. The only limitations we have are the ones we set ourselves, and I constantly remind myself of that.

How can your professors help make the transition back to 'student' a little smoother for other students like you?

I think professors who set clear rules and expectations in the beginning, who are accommodating by answering questions after class or during office hours, and professors who care about their students make for a smooth transition and an overall successful college experience for their students.

How have your professors motivated you (anything they said, how they treated you, encouraged the class as a whole, etc.)?

I've been lucky, in a sense, to have some 'bad' teachers in the past, because I know now what I would call a 'good' teacher. In my experience, the best professors have motivated me to never give up, by watching how passionate they are when they teach and by instilling confidence in me. Throughout the semester they reassured me that I was good enough and that anything is possible.

How have your professors made a difference for you? Are there any ways they may have helped that they're not be aware of?

I missed the first week of my summer Statistics class because of a health issue. I communicated that through email with my professor. I was certain that I would be too far behind and that I would have to drop the class, but to my surprise my professor was so empathetic and accommodating. My professor empathized with

me and caught me up with the topics I missed.
Because of him I was motivated to continue on
in the class and pass with a B, which resulted in
me graduating!

**What type of classroom environment and/or
setup do you think made learning most
effective for you and other students
(professor attributes, lectures, activities,
exams, hands on learning, any other methods
of teaching and learning that you like in
particular)?**
I think a professor's enthusiasm is key. I enjoy
taking notes/ following along in lecture, and I
think worksheets after each lecture are very
helpful, especially with hands-on learning.

**What do you hope to get out of going back to
college?**
I hope to gain as much knowledge as possible
and to graduate with my second degree in A.S.
Nursing!

*Now go give yourself a pat on the back! It
looks like happy, helpful professors are
inspiring their students and making a good
name for the colleges they work at.*

Commonly Asked Questions

Q: How can I teach college part-time?

If you have a master's degree, you can get a job teaching at the college level. Call the community colleges in your area to find out when they hold adjunct interviews. The interviews are usually pretty laid back, with a convenient meeting place on campus for everyone who may be interested. The only requirement to teach is a master's degree-teaching experience preferred, but not required. Other times, searching for open adjunct positions on an employment website and submitting the required documents is enough to get you the job. I've been hired both ways.

Q: How do I get teaching experience?

Your best bet is to find out how to become a Teacher's Assistant while you're getting your master's degree (if you ask around the department and put in some work to qualify, usually you'll be given the opportunity to be a TA- at least that's how it worked at my school). After grad school, it's harder to find opportunities teaching at the college level, which makes it difficult to then go on and teach as an adjunct, but definitely not impossible.

I know quite a few people who were hired to teach without traditional teaching experience, and it's because they had a master's and worked in administration or student services at a particular community or state college. So if you get your foot in the door and get to know the right people at the school, you may get the chance to teach.

Q: Can I teach any class if I have a master's degree?

You can only teach classes that are related to your master's degree. For instance, someone with a communication degree can teach public speaking, mass media, interpersonal communication, communication theories, etc. Someone with a business degree can teach general business, microeconomics, macroeconomics, marketing, etc.

If you'd like to teach something that's unrelated to your master's degree, you can take 18 credits worth of master's classes (at whatever school you choose- but remember, this can be pretty expensive) in the area you're interested in teaching, which qualifies you to then teach college level classes in that subject.

Q: Can I teach as an adjunct if I also have a full-time job?

Many of the part-time college instructors I've met have traditional 9 to 5 jobs during the day and teach one evening class a week at a local college for fun, so you can absolutely do this in your free time for some extra income.

Q: Do adjuncts get to choose their own schedule?

The easy answer is yes, you get to choose your own schedule. However, sometimes it depends on the school. I work at 2 schools that book me at the same day and time each semester (based on the times I specified would work for me during my first semester with them), but they always double check with me before they make anything official, which is a nice courtesy (not every school does this). I guarantee they also would work with me if I needed to completely change my schedule.

Another school I work at mixes it up, which is kind of fun. I usually keep my evenings free for them each semester because I never know what night they'll have a class available for me. Eventually you figure out how each college operates so you never end up double-booking yourself by accident.

Q: How do I know if there are community colleges in my area looking for instructors?

There are community colleges all over the country, and I'll bet there are at least a couple within a reasonable driving distance from you. It's not too hard to find an available adjunct opening, either. Each time I check the 'Employment' section of various college websites, there are a number of positions available, so you won't have a problem finding teaching opportunities (it's the full-time opportunities that are harder to come by).

Q: What time of year should I apply for adjunct positions and how long should I expect to wait until I hear back?

Summer is the best time to apply for adjunct positions because there's a lot of turnover in the adjunct world, and the fall semester is when student enrollment is at its highest. However, any time during the year is fine.

As far as actually getting the job and the typical waiting period, it varies. Over the years I've applied during the summer months to teach part-time at a total of 8 local schools, and it was hit or miss. I never heard back from 4 of the schools where I applied, but the other 4 responded almost immediately or within a month.

Q: How can I teach online?

In my experience, I've taught face-to-face classes for the school for about a year before I started teaching online for them. Each school has a different certification to teach online, and each college uses a different system to run their online classes (which is why they have school-specific certification courses).

The best way to get into teaching online is by looking into the college website's 'Faculty' tab once you're hired by the school, and signing up for the certification class. You can also email the department secretary, or someone involved with faculty development, to ask about online opportunities if you can't find the information online. Once you follow the steps required by the particular college, you'll be able to teach online as soon as you tell them you're ready and they approve of the course you've developed.

Q: Are there opportunities for advancement as a part-time instructor?

Adjunct instructors don't get raises based on performance or how long they've been with the school. However, being an adjunct can definitely help when you apply for full-time positions that might become available at the college. Not only do you have the experience they're looking for, but the people who matter in the hiring process are usually familiar with you, so that gives you an edge over any outside applicants.

Q: Can I really live on an adjunct salary if I want that to be my 'full-time' job?

It can definitely be done. However, you have to be very mindful of your spending, you'll have to pay for your own health benefits (these are not provided to part-time college employees), and you'll need to be okay living a simpler life. I imagine it's pretty manageable when you're single, and would be much more difficult if you have children. If your significant other is okay being the breadwinner, then you're good to go.

Q: I've heard some negative things about teaching part-time. How can someone remain positive as an adjunct?

I believe the negativity comes from people who, understandably, would prefer a full-time teaching job and benefits. Occasionally, a school will drop all the classes an adjunct is scheduled to teach at the last minute, usually without giving notice (this happens to me about once every two years) because of unexpected low student enrollment. When this happens, it makes adjuncts feel vulnerable and taken advantage of, especially when they rely on the income from those classes.

The way I've remained positive is by providing myself with my own job security. I work at 4 schools and I teach online and face-to-face, so there's always a place for me at at least 3 of the schools, even if one falls through at the last minute. It can be difficult to be proactive about this, but you learn to be prepared and just go with it. I still get to be in the classroom, and that's what it's all about for me.

Q: What kinds of things can I implement in the classroom to make it a more positive experience? How can I motivate my students?

First, I respect my students, which makes for a great, supportive environment for everyone. Using video clips during lecture to liven things up and keeping things relevant to their generation helps them to stay engaged and excited about learning, which will make you a pretty happy professor.

Q: Are there any resources you would suggest for professors and/or for college students?

Over the years I've found quite a few websites and books that have really helped me and my students along the way, below are my favorites:

Communitycollegesuccess.com
Community College Success by Isa Adney
Ellenbremen.com ('The Chatty Professor')
Khanacademy.org
TED.com
The Happiness Advantage by Shawn Achor

Q: How can I contact you?

Feel free to contact me using the form within the 'Contact' tab on the happyprofessor.com website, or email me directly at erin@happyprofessor.com. I'll be happy to answer any questions you have.

About the Author

Erin Ebanks is the adjunct professor behind the website happyprofessor.com where she writes about student success, classroom tips, and enjoying life. She teaches a number of online and face-to-face classes each semester, ranging from Intro to Communication to Family Communication.

At 23, Erin taught her first college course while in grad school, and never looked back. Five years later, she's still finding new ways to connect with students and make life worthwhile, from spending quite some time in the classroom and most of her free time doing anything outdoors- even if that means grading online assignments outside the local coffee shop.

Erin has a B.A. in Communication from Stetson University in Deland, Florida, and an M.S. in Mass Media Communication from the University of Central Florida in Orlando, Florida.

Made in the USA
Middletown, DE
01 June 2022